AF006966

# Dick Whittington

## A Basic Pantomime in Three Acts

### Trudy West

A Samuel French Acting Edition

FOUNDED 1830

SAMUELFRENCH-LONDON.CO.UK
SAMUELFRENCH.COM

Copyright © 1959 by Trudy West
All Rights Reserved

*DICK WHITTINGTON* is fully protected under the copyright laws of the British Commonwealth, including Canada, the United States of America, and all other countries of the Copyright Union. All rights, including professional and amateur stage productions, recitation, lecturing, public reading, motion picture, radio broadcasting, television and the rights of translation into foreign languages are strictly reserved.

ISBN 978-0-573-06420-3

www.samuelfrench-london.co.uk

www.samuelfrench.com

---

### For Amateur Production Enquiries

### United Kingdom and World excluding North America

plays@SamuelFrench-London.co.uk

020 7255 4302/01

Each title is subject to availability from Samuel French, depending upon country of performance.

---

CAUTION: Professional and amateur producers are hereby warned that *DICK WHITTINGTON* is subject to a licensing fee. Publication of this play does not imply availability for performance. Both amateurs and professionals considering a production are strongly advised to apply to the appropriate agent before starting rehearsals, advertising, or booking a theatre. A licensing fee must be paid whether the title is presented for charity or gain and whether or not admission is charged.

The professional rights in this play are controlled by Samuel French Ltd, 52 Fitzroy Street, London, W1T 5JR.

No one shall make any changes in this title for the purpose of production. No part of this book may be reproduced, stored in a retrieval system, or transmitted in any form, by any means, now known or yet to be invented, including mechanical, electronic, photocopying, recording, videotaping, or otherwise, without the prior written permission of the publisher. No one shall upload this title, or part of this title, to any social media websites.

The right of Trudy West to be identified as author of this work has been asserted by him in accordance with Section 77 of the Copyright, Designs and Patents Act 1988

# CHARACTERS

*(in the order of their appearance)*

HARRY \} Cockneys
HARRIET /
KITTY, chief parlour-maid to Fitzwarren
FREDERICK, chief clerk to Fitzwarren
DICK WHITTINGTON
SUKIE, the cat
PANSY, the cook
BOTTLE, the butler
ALDERMAN FITZWARREN, a merchant
ALICE, his daughter
PERCY PILBEAM, a merchant
PING \} attendants to the King and Queen
PONG /
CAPTAIN BILGE
KING BANGA-BANGA \} of the Boko Islands
QUEEN CLANGA-CLANGA /
CHORUS OF COCKNEYS, REVELLERS, SERVANTS, CLERKS, MAIDS, MERCHANTS, WIVES, NATIVES AND SAILORS

# SYNOPSIS OF SCENES

## ACT I

SCENE 1  *A London Street*
SCENE 2  *The Kitchen in Fitzwarren's House*
SCENE 3  *Fitzwarren's Warehouse*
SCENE 4  *On the Road*

## ACT II

SCENE 1  *Fitzwarren's Warehouse*
SCENE 2  *The Deck of the "Saucy Sally"*
SCENE 3  *The Boko Islands*

## ACT III

SCENE 1  *Fitzwarren's Warehouse*
SCENE 2  *The same*

## MUSICAL NUMBERS

### ACT I

SCENE 1
1. Opening Chorus and Dance — REVELLERS
2. Song — DICK
2a. Reprise of No. 1 — REVELLERS

SCENE 2
3. Song, with Chorus — KITTY and SERVANTS
4. Ensemble Chorus — PANSY, BOTTLE, FREDERICK, KITTY and SERVANTS
5. Duet — ALICE and DICK

SCENE 3
6. Trio and Chorus — FREDERICK, CLERKS and MAIDS
7. Quartette — FITZWARREN, PERCY, PANSY and BOTTLE
8. Duet — ALICE and DICK
8a. Reprise of No. 6 — FREDERICK, KITTY, CLERKS and MAIDS

SCENE 4
9. Song, *Bow Bells* — DICK (with unseen Chorus)

### ACT II

SCENE 1
10. Ensemble — MERCHANTS and LADIES
11. Duet — PING, PONG and COMPANY
12. Duet — FREDERICK and KITTY
13. Duet — ALICE and DICK
14. Ensemble — The COMPANY
INTERLUDE
14a. Reprise of No. 13 — ALICE and DICK

## MUSICAL NUMBERS

SCENE 2
- 15 Ensemble — SAILORS
- 16 Duet — DICK *and* CAPTAIN
- 16a Reprise of No. 13 — DICK
- 17 Ensemble — The COMPANY
- INTERLUDE
- 18 Song — ALICE

SCENE 3
- 19 Duet — KING *and* QUEEN (*with* Dance of NATIVES)
- 20 Song — PANSY
- 21 Ensemble — The COMPANY
- 22 Ballet of RATS
- 23 Song — ALICE
- 24 Chorus — KING, PANSY, BOTTLE *and* NATIVES
- 24a Reprise of No. 21 — The COMPANY

# ACT III

SCENE 1
- 25 Ensemble — FREDERICK, KITTY, CLERKS *and* MAIDS
- 25a Reprise of No. 23 — ALICE
- 26 Ensemble — The COMPANY
- INTERLUDE
- 27 Speciality Number — PERCY *and* DANCING GIRLS

SCENE 2
- 28 Trio. Reprise of No. 6 — FREDERICK *and* CLERKS
- 29 Duet — ALICE *and* DICK
- 30 Grand Finale — FULL COMPANY

# DICK WHITTINGTON

## ACT I

### Scene 1

SCENE—*Outside Alderman Fitzwarren's house in Golden Square, London. New Year's Eve.*
*A street cloth at the back. Wings to mask in. Up* R, *steps and a portico, leading into the house. A mounting-block down* L.

*When the* CURTAIN *rises, a number of* REVELLERS, *led by* HARRY *and* HARRIET, *are entering* R *and* L. *They are in festive mood, carrying bladders on sticks, long feathers, etc., and wear comic hats or masks. They sing and dance a rollicking number.*

No. 1 *Opening Number and Dance* (REVELLERS)

(*After the Number, they hail* KITTY *and* FREDERICK *who enter* L. KITTY *is a pretty, vivacious girl, very flirtatious.* FREDERICK *is a jaunty young man, also very inclined to flirtation*)

KITTY (*moves* C) What a wonderful evening it's been, Frederick.

(KITTY *and* FREDERICK *kiss. Catcalls come from the* REVELLERS)

FREDERICK. Yes—there's something *about* New Year's Eve . . .

KITTY. There's *romance* in the air!

(*They kiss again. There are catcalls and whistles from the* REVELLERS)

HARRY. Go on—give the lady a smacker!
HARRIET. Tell her she's yer Donah!

(KITTY *and* FREDERICK *turn and see the Revellers*)

KITTY. Frederick—send them away.
FREDERICK (*to the Revellers; ineffectually*) Go away.

HARRY. 'Oo d'yer fink you are?
KITTY. If you want to know, I'm Kitty, Alderman Fitzwarren's head parlour-maid.
FREDERICK. And I—am Frederick Filer, his chief clerk.
HARRY (*affectedly*) An' Ay'm 'Arry 'Iggins of Lambeff.
HARRIET. 'Arriet 'Oskins of the same! Old Fitz-who's-it lives 'ere, don't 'e?
FREDERICK. He does. A most respected merchant of the city.
KITTY. Who won't be at all pleased when he returns from the Guildhall New Year's Ball, to see riffraff on his doorstep. (*She makes a grimace at them*)
HARRY. Garn! It's New Year's Eve for us, too!
HARRIET. Give your face an 'oliday and laugh fer once!

(*The* REVELLERS *cheer.*
DICK WHITTINGTON *and his cat,* SUKIE, *enter* L. DICK *is shabbily dressed, with a pack on his shoulder. He looks tired and travel-stained. He and* SUKIE *stand looking at the others, who are intent on Frederick and Kitty*)

DICK. Excuse me . . .
HARRY (*to Frederick*) Give 'er another, mate!
DICK. Excuse me . . .

(ALL *turn and look at Dick*)

HARRY. 'Ullo, 'ullo! Where you spring from, young shaver?
HARRIET. 'Oo are *you*, if it's not a rude answer?
DICK. My name is Dick Whittington and this is my cat, Sukie.

(SUKIE *bows two or three times. The others react*)

We've tramped all the way from the West Country to find work in London. This is London, isn't it?
HARRIET. London? I fink so! (*To Harry, with a wink*) This is London, in't it, 'Arry?
HARRY. Well, I may be mistook, but I've alwiz thought it was the last firty years!

(*General laugh*)

FREDERICK. Of course it's London.

DICK. Then please direct me to the streets that are paved with gold. I was told they were here—in the City . . .

(*The* CROWD *roars. Ad lib.:* "*Paved with gold! Ever 'ear anything like it? That's a good 'un!*" *etc. etc.*)

KITTY. Oh, poor boy—don't laugh at him!

DICK. But aren't they? In my village, everyone thinks the London streets are paved with gold.

HARRY. Wouldja berleeve it!

HARRIET. Someone's bin 'avin' you on, ducks!

FREDERICK. This street is Golden Square. Perhaps that's what they meant.

DICK. Perhaps. I'm looking for work—is there any work to be had round here?

HARRIET. Work? Never 'eard of it!

HARRY. Don't talk about work, mate, on New Year's Eve!

FREDERICK. Alderman Fitzwarren, who lives here, is a demon for work. You ask him—in the morning.

DICK. Oh, I will—I will!

HARRY. Meantime—forget unpleasant subjicks in a bit of song and dance! (*He slaps Dick on the back*)

(DICK *staggers and subsides to a mounting-block down* L., *where he sits. At the same time the* REVELLERS, KITTY *and* FREDERICK *sing a Reprise of No. 1.*
*As the Number ends, New Year bells peal out. There are ad lib. shouts:* "*Happy New Year!*" *etc., as the* REVELLERS *dance off* R *and* L.
FREDERICK *and* KITTY *exit into the house, up* R. DICK *and* SUKIE *are left alone*)

DICK. Happy New Year, Sukie—Happy New Year! I wonder if it will be happy for us? We've come a long way in search of a fortune, you and I. We're tired—hungry—strangers in a great strange city of our dreams. (*He rises, a little stiff and weak, and moves* C) We've no-one but each other, Sukie, no-one at all. It's dark, and cold —but never mind—in the morning—there'll be another day.

(SUKIE *comes to him*)

(*He strokes the cat*) You'll see! You'll see! (*He sings*)

No. 2   *Song* (DICK)
(Tune: *Evening Song*)

Poor and lone am I,
Far from home and kindred,
Ne'er a place to lie
Rest my weary head.
People hurry by,
Stranger lone they do not heed,
Still my cat have I—
A friend indeed!

2

City of my dreams
Ends the last long weary mile,
Paved with gold, it seems
Fortune's in your smile!
Now the glad New Year
Bids me lift my heart again,
Hope shall conquer fear
My goal to attain!

(As DICK *finishes the Number he staggers a little*)

Oh, Sukie, I can't see! It's all—going round—and round! (*He gropes his way to the portico*) Sukie—stay by me . . .

(DICK *collapses on the steps of the house.* SUKIE *settles by him, miaouwing.*
    *A few* REVELLERS *cross over from* R *to* L *waving balloons, etc., but all ignore Dick.*
    PANSY *and* BOTTLE *enter* L, *singing* "*Happy Birthday to You*". *Pansy is a typical Dame and dressed in a weird assortment of clothes. Bottle is in butler's uniform. He is*

habitually miserable, but at the moment both are a little "merry")

PANSY (suddenly stopping singing) Why are we singing that, Bottle? It's nobody's birthday, is it?

BOTTLE. 'Course it is! It's the New Year's birthday. Perhaps I'll be in the New Year's honours list—Borren Battle!

PANSY. If you're a Baron, I'm a marshmallow!

BOTTLE. And you'll come to a sticky finish! (*He laughs loudly and digs her in the ribs*) Pie-eyed Pansy—the Alderman's Cook! (*He laughs*)

(PANSY *tries to kick Bottle in the rear and misses, nearly falling*)

PANSY. Stick to your buttling, Bottle, and I'll stick to my frying-pan!

BOTTLE. And what a sight for sore eyes that'd be! (*Singing raucously*) "We'll all stick together like the *ivy*, on the old garden wall."

PANSY. Call that singing? I'll show you how to warble—follow me!

BOTTLE. Where?

PANSY. Open your throttle, Bottle—like this!

(PANSY *bawls out a few bars of a popular song while* BOTTLE *cringes, holding his hands over his ears. They go up* R *to the portico and see Dick and Sukie*)

Coo! Look what's the cat's brought in!

BOTTLE (*peering at Dick*) It's a bundle o' rags!

PANSY. Leave it—come inside and have some black coffee. It won't take me a minute to take me coat off and put the coffee-pot on.

(PANSY *exits at the side of the house*)

BOTTLE (*following*) All right—all right! The Alderman can move the rubbish!

(BOTTLE *follows Pansy off. Some* REVELLERS *cross over, singing and laughing and exit.*

ALDERMAN FITZWARREN *and his daughter,* ALICE,

*enter L.* FITZWARREN *is a kindly man of middle age, quietly dressed, with an air of prosperity.* ALICE *is young and pretty, and very attached to her father*)

FITZWARREN (*as they enter*) Well, Alice my dear, I'm glad you enjoyed the ball.

ALICE. It was *lovely*, Father. I enjoyed every minute of it!

FITZWARREN. Young Pilbeam was taking a good deal of notice of you, eh? (*He pats her shoulder and laughs indulgently*)

ALICE (*casually*) Oh, we happened to dance well together, that's all. Our steps fitted in.

FITZWARREN. Well, it's a good enough start. His father's one of the richest merchants in the City. Percy will inherit a fine business one day.

ALICE (*indifferently*) Will he? Then he'll need to cultivate a little more common sense if he's to manage it.

FITZWARREN. He showed remarkable common sense in *one* direction tonight, anyway.

ALICE (*yawning*) Oh, I'm *so* tired, but it's been a wonderful start to the New Year!

FITZWARREN (*tenderly*) Has it, my dear? Then I'm glad. We'll get along in now—time for bed.

(*They move to the porch and stop suddenly as they see Dick*)

Bless my soul! Who's this curled up in my doorway?

ALICE (*with quick sympathy*) Oh, it's a poor boy! (*She kneels beside Dick*)

(SUKIE *watches and purrs*)

I think he's fainted! (*She fans him gently*)

FITZWARREN. Be careful, Alice! It may be a trick to gain sympathy.

ALICE. I'm sure it's not, Father. See how pale and ill he looks! Oh, I believe he's reviving a little.

(DICK *begins to move and open his eyes.* SUKIE *mews loudly and walks about agitatedly*)

FITZWARREN. A cat with him, too! Well, well!

(ALICE *strokes Sukie gently*)

ALICE. Poor pussy! What's the matter, then? Are you hungry?

(SUKIE *begs*. DICK *sits up and looks about him*)

FITZWARREN. Well, young man, what's the meaning of this, eh? It's against the law to sleep on doorsteps, you know.

DICK. I'm sorry, sir. I must have—fainted. (*He struggles to his feet and leans against a pillar for support*)

(SUKIE *rubs round him*)

ALICE. Oh, poor boy! Please let us help him, Father!

FITZWARREN. H'rrrm! (*To Dick*) What's your name, boy, and where do you come from?

DICK. My name is Dick Whittington and I come from a village in the West Country. I walked to London to find a fortune, sir.

FITZWARREN. Nobody makes a fortune honestly without *working* for it.

DICK. I *want* work, sir. I will do *anything*.

ALICE. Oh, Father, I believe cook wants a boy in the kitchen.

FITZWARREN. We'll see about it—we'll see. (*Kindly, to Dick*) You'd better come into the house, my lad. You need food, and a rest.

(*As he turns to go in by the door,* ALICE *and* DICK *look at each other. He smiles, and she looks away shyly*)

DICK (*to Fitzwarren; tentatively*) I cannot leave my faithful cat, sir . . .

FITZWARREN. Bring him in, boy, bring him in!

ALICE. Of course!

FITZWARREN, ALICE *and* DICK *exit to the house.*

SUKIE *purrs loudly, does a few comical dance steps, then runs in after them.*

*The* REVELLERS *enter* R *and* L *and sing a Reprise of No. 1.*

*The* TABS *close*

*The* REVELLERS *continue the Number ad lib. in front of the* TABS *during the scene change.*

## SCENE 2

SCENE—*The Kitchen in Alderman Fitzwarren's house. The next morning.*
　　*There is a large kitchen table* L, *a range back* C *and a cupboard up* R. *There are exits* R *and down* L.

*When the* TABS *open a number of* MANSERVANTS *and* MAID-SERVANTS *are on stage, with* KITTY. *All wear aprons and carry dusters, brooms, brushes, etc., ready for work.*

　　No. 3　*Song with Chorus* (KITTY *and* SERVANTS)

*As the Number ends,* FREDERICK *enters* R, *and looks at them all in disgust.*

FREDERICK. What's going on here? Such a din—I can't study the stocks and shares!
KITTY. Then we'll give you some shocks and stares for a change!

　　(FREDERICK *moans and holds his head*)

A MAN. We're celebrating!
FREDERICK. Not *again!* I haven't got over last night's revels yet.
ALL (*reprovingly*) Oooh!
KITTY. *That* was New Year's Eve—*this* is New Year's Day!
FREDERICK. There ought to be six months between them.
KITTY. Misery! Your idea of a romantic evening is to sit in front of the fire cuddling a ledger!
FREDERICK. A *lodger?*
KITTY. *Ledger!*
FREDERICK (*holding his head*) Don't *shout*.
A MAN. He's got a hangover!
A GIRL. Poor old Frederick!

　　(*They all laugh*)

KITTY. We've got to make good resolutions today.
ALL (*ad lib.*) Hooray! Less work and more play! What about a rise? (*Etc. etc.*)
FREDERICK (*grumpily*) I shall resolve not to make any resolutions.
KITTY. And *I* shall resolve not to talk to crotchety clerks! (*She flounces away from Frederick*)
ALL (*derisively*) Hear, hear!
FREDERICK. Oh, but Kitty dear, I did want to say something *most* important!

(KITTY *is mollified and sidles back to him*)

KITTY (*very sweetly*) M'yes? Tell me.
FREDERICK. Could you get me a couple of aspirins?

(KITTY *turns angrily, stamping her foot. The others laugh*)

KITTY. Aspirins!

(KITTY *goes to flounce off through the exit* L *and collides with* PANSY, *who is entering.* PANSY *looks as if she has had a night out*)

PANSY (*holding her ribs*) Ow! You've dented me chassis!
KITTY. Sorry! I'm in a hurry.
PANSY. Can't wait to get at your work, I suppose?

(FREDERICK *laughs, then holds his head in sudden agony.* BOTTLE *enters down* R)

KITTY (*looking at him*) Aspirins! Oh!

(KITTY *goes to rush off down* R, *and collides with* BOTTLE, *upsetting his pompous progress*)

BOTTLE. Now then, now then! (*He catches hold of Kitty and looks at her*) Capering Kitty again!
KITTY (*furiously*) Yes, Mr Bottle. You'll know me next time you see me, won't you?
BOTTLE (*darkly*) There won't be a next time if I have any more sauce from you, my girl!
PANSY (*bustling to the table*) Sauce! That reminds me! We'll all set to and peel that barrelful of onions.

(ALL *back away, alarmed*)

BOTTLE. Wait a minute—wait a minute, Madam Picklejoy, please! I give the orders around here.

PANSY (*menacingly*) You, and who else?

BOTTLE (*hastily*) Er—you, of course.

PANSY. So long as we all know!

BOTTLE (*to the Servants*) Come on, jump to it! Line up and form fours by twos.

(*The* SERVANTS *shuffle their feet and slope their brooms and brushes over their shoulders*)

Now, listen! Housemaids—dust, sweep . . .

PANSY. And don't tickle him!

BOTTLE. Parlour-maids—parleyvoo in the parlour, with *me!*

(KITTY *wriggles and giggles coquettishly.* FREDERICK *glares.*

DICK *enters* L., *with* SUKIE)

DICK (*to Bottle; briskly*) Good morning! Are you Bottle, the butler?

(BOTTLE *turns, amazed*)

BOTTLE (*with hauteur*) *Mr* Bottle to you!

DICK. Splendid! Where's the cook?

PANSY (*bridling*) Ay 'ave the *h*onour to be Meddem Pansy Picklejoy, catering h'operative in chief to this 'ere maynarge.

(SUKIE *gives a very loud miaouw.* DICK *grins and the others giggle*)

FREDERICK. Blow me down if it isn't the boy we saw last night!

KITTY. *And* his cat!

(SUKIE *goes to* KITTY *purring, and she pats him*)

Nice pussy, then!

FREDERICK. Lucky cat!

BOTTLE (*very severely; to Dick*) And *who*, might I make so bold to ask, are you, young man?
PANSY. If you're a new deterrent, I don't want any.
DICK. I'm Dick Whittington, and this is Sukie, my cat.

(SUKIE *bows to them all*)
I've come to London to make my fortune.

(*The others laugh*)
PANSY. Some mothers do 'ave 'em, don't they?
DICK. Alderman Fitzwarren has been very kind to me. He said I may work for him.
BOTTLE (*sourly*) Very kind, I'm sure. And who's going to be saddled with the likes o' you?
DICK (*brightly*) *You* are!

(PANSY *and* BOTTLE *react*)
I'm the new cook's boy!
PANSY. Well, clout me with a cleaver! *I* don't want you!
DICK. Sorry—boss's orders. And Sukie's to be chief rat-catcher.
BOTTLE (*venomously*) I'll give you *work!* Listen to us!

(*The* SERVANTS *form up and march round the stage as they sing*)
No. 4 *Ensemble Chorus* (PANSY, BOTTLE, FREDERICK, KITTY *and* SERVANTS)

(*After the Number they exit down* R, FREDERICK *staggering off last.* PANSY, BOTTLE, DICK *and* SUKIE *are left on stage.* PANSY *opens the cupboard door, unhooks a large slab of "pastry", slaps it on the table and begins to roll it out.* BOTTLE *starts to polish a tankard, very slowly. Both ignore Dick. Pansy goes on humming the last refrain as she slaps the pastry, hanging a surplus piece round her neck*)

DICK (*after a pause*) Er—excuse me . . .
PANSY (*ignoring him*) Nice hop last night, eh, Bottle? Thought I should have died laughing when you swallowed your squeaker! Fair black in the face, you was!

BOTTLE. Every time I took a deep breath last night I got up and oiled meself!

PANSY. And you were well oiled already.

(BOTTLE *breathes hard on the silver and polishes.* DICK *tries again*)

DICK. Can I help?

BOTTLE (*to Pansy*) I saw *you* eating the candles off the cake and setting light to the celery!

PANSY. Coo! I thought it had a funny flavour!

DICK (*a little louder*) Excuse me . . .

(SUKIE *miaouws.*
 ALICE *and* FITZWARREN *enters* LC)

ALICE. Good morning, Cook! Good morning, Bottle!

PANSY } (*chanting loudly; together*) Good morning, Mr
BOTTLE } Alderman!

(BOTTLE *polishes frantically and* PANSY *slaps and rolls at a terrific rate*)

FITZWARREN (*to Dick*) I see you've introduced yourself, my boy.

ALICE. I hope you feel better this morning, Dick. Did you sleep well?

DICK. Yes, thank you, Miss Alice. I was very comfortable.

(SUKIE *goes to* ALICE *and she fondles him*)

FITZWARREN. Good! Good! What has Cook given you to do?

BOTTLE (*pointedly*) We don't really *need* another pair of hands, so to speak, miss.

ALICE. Nonsense, Bottle! Dick is willing to do anything, aren't you, Dick?

DICK. Yes, Miss Alice.

PANSY. Good! There's a barrelful of onions waiting to be peeled for pickling.

ALICE. Oh!

(FITZWARREN *looks at Dick, watching his reaction*)

FITZWARREN. Well? What do you say to that, Dick?
DICK (*cheerfully*) I've said I'm willing to do anything, sir.
FITZWARREN (*patting him on the shoulder*) Bravo! You'll do, my boy!
PANSY. He certainly knows his onions.
BOTTLE (*as he passes Dick*) "If you have tears, prepare to shed them now."
FITZWARREN (*to Alice*) I'll leave you to settle these domestic details, my dear. If you want me, I shall be in the counting-house.
ALICE. Very well, Father.

(FITZWARREN *exits* L. SUKIE *begs to Alice*)

Oh, clever Sukie! She's asking for a job, too!
PANSY (*slapping pastry viciously*) There's no room for a cat here while *I'm* about!
BOTTLE. 'Sright. Turn him out!
DICK (*going to Sukie protectively*) My cat stays where I stay.
ALICE (*to Dick*) Of course!
PANSY. It's that cat or me! This is *my* kitchen!
ALICE (*with spirit*) And it's *my* father's *house!* You take your orders from *me!*
BOTTLE. Well! What a to-do over a perishin' puss.
ALICE (*rounding on him*) And the same goes for you, Bottle.
PANSY. Hoity-toity! Oh, to think I dandled a viper in my bosom on my knee!
BOTTLE (*shaking his head*) Proper little party piece, ain't she?
ALICE. Don't try to take advantage of being old servants! You've *got* to accept Dick Whittington *and* his cat. If you don't treat him fairly, I shall tell father to dismiss you both.
DICK (*uncomfortably*) Oh, please—Miss Alice . . .
PANSY. All right, all right, all right! I'll go and pack me things now! (*She flounces to the exit* L)
BOTTLE. I'm with you, Madam Picklejoy. I'm out in sympathy!

(PANSY *and* BOTTLE *exit* L. DICK *turns to Alice, very perturbed*)

DICK. Miss Alice! What have you done?
ALICE (*laughing*) That's all right, Dick!
DICK. But they said they were going to leave.
ALICE. They've said that at least once a month ever since I can remember.
DICK. You are so kind—I don't want to cause trouble in your home.
ALICE (*fondling Sukie*) I'll see there's no trouble.
DICK. But if the servants don't like Sukie or me?
ALICE. They'll soon learn to like you both.
DICK (*impulsively*) You are so good, and so—so beautiful!
ALICE. Do you *want* to stay here, Dick?
DICK. More than anything else on earth!
ALICE (*a little shyly*) Why—that's splendid! (*To Sukie*) And what about you, Sukie?

(SUKIE *rubs round her, purring*)

DICK. Sukie's saying "yes", too. We couldn't be parted, Miss Alice. The cat is all I've got.
ALICE. You won't be parted. I promise you that.
DICK. And I promise I'll work and work to repay you and your father for giving me this chance. Some day, perhaps, I'll be a great citizen of London—powerful and rich, and it will be because *you* helped me.

(*They move together and sing*)

No. 5 *Duet* (ALICE *and* DICK)

INTERLUDE *in front of* TABS *during Scene Change Suggested Number:*

*Duet* (BOTTLE *and* PANSY, *with* CHORUS)

## Scene 3

Scene—*The Warehouse of Alderman Fitzwarren's establishment.*

*The setting is an interior cloth at the back with wings to mask in. There are three desks and high stools. One is up* C, *facing the wall. The others are* R *and* L *respectively, facing the side walls, and these also have high stools. There may be a bale of cloth down* R, *and another—or a crate—down* L, *which may be used as seats. There are exits* R *and* L.

*When the* Curtain *rises, the stage is empty except for* Frederick *and two* Clerks. Frederick *is seated on the high stool, back* C, *facing the "wall". The* Clerks *are also seated facing their walls,* R *and* L, *so that their backs are also to the audience. They are writing most industriously with their quills, turning over pages of ledgers, etc., while the music of one verse of the Number is being played very softly indeed. On the last note,* Frederick *turns on his stool, and comes down stage to the intro. music with stealthy steps, pausing for one beat on each step.*

No. 6   Trio and Chorus (Frederick *and* Clerks—*with Dance of* Clerks *and* Maids)
(Tune: *Drink, Puppy, Drink*)

Frederick. Life's rather dark
   For a linen draper's clerk,
   All day keeping books with precision.
Clerks (*shouting; without turning*)
   Precision!
Frederick. He's not paid enough—
Clerks (*turning*)
   For to keep himself in snuff!
Frederick. So perforce he is a source of derision!
Clerks (*imitating satirical laughter*)
   Ha-ha-ha-ha-ha-ha-ha!

(*The* Clerks *slip off their stools and join Frederick*)

|          | REFRAIN |
|---|---|
| ALL. | We don't like the air |
|  | Of the City's Golden Square, |
|  | We'd prefer the atmosphere of Ar*cady!* |
| CLERK (R) | It is said that in the glades |
| CLERK (L) | Are a host of fairy maids! |
| ALL. | And each guaranteed "quite the lady"! |

(ALL *dance round the stage like fairies, scattering flowers* R *and* L, *to the music of Mendelssohn's "Spring Song". They finish* C, *and sing the following repeat of the refrain*)

ALL.   'Til that happy day
       We must manage on our pay
       As we keep Fitzwarren's books with precision!

(*Pause, as* FREDERICK *sings on a descending scale to a very deep note, anxiously watched by the others*)

FREDERICK. Pre-ci-hi-hi-hi-hision!
CLERK (R)  Though we ponder and regret—
CLERK (L)  That we cannot quite forget—
ALL.       The Fairymaids and glades in our vision!
           (*Spoken*) Aaah—*me!*

(*The Chorus of* PARLOUR-MAIDS *and* CLERKS *enter, to the music of "Spring Song" and all dance, led by* KITTY *and* FREDERICK *as principal dancers.
    This is interrupted by the entrance of* BOTTLE, *who is raging*)

BOTTLE. That's enough! That's enough of the high jinks, thank you!
FREDERICK. Tra-la-la to you!

(FREDERICK *twirls* KITTY *towards him and kisses her lightly. She pirouettes back and kisses* BOTTLE *impudently. He is horrified, and scrubs his face with his hand*)

BOTTLE. Shameless hussy! Do that once more . . .
KITTY. Not likely. (*She pirouettes back to Frederick*)

SCENE 3      DICK WHITTINGTON        17

(*The dance is resumed in which* BOTTLE *joins, as if in a trance.*
DICK *enters* L. BOTTLE *catches sight of Dick and detaches himself. The dance stops*)

BOTTLE. Ah! And you're another! Back to the kitchen, what are you doing here, no excuses, so shut up when I'm talking, I never heard of such . . . Why don't you answer?

(DICK *throws out his hands in despair*)

Wait till Cook sees you.

(PANSY *strides in* L, *rolling-pin in hand*)

PANSY. Who's talking about me may I ask?
BOTTLE (*pointing at Dick*) He is!
PANSY. How dare he even open his mouth? (*To Dick*) Back to your work, scullion! Have you drawn the Alderman's bath?
DICK. Yes.
PANSY. Then rub it out again.
DICK. Too late—he's had it.
PANSY. Then so have you! He'll be down the moment he's dry!
FREDERICK. Clerks—to your work! Unload the bales and crates!
PANSY. Girls—to your work! Forget about your dates!

(ALL *dance "Spring Song" as before, which takes* FREDERICK, KITTY, *the* MAIDS *and* CLERKS *off* R *and* L. BOTTLE *and* PANSY *stop dancing as the others exit.* DICK *approaches them*)

DICK. *Now* perhaps you'll let *me* speak!
BOTTLE. Not till you're spoken *to*, young shaver!
PANSY. And not then if I knows it!
DICK. I refuse to be bullied like this!
BOTTLE. Getting uppity, eh?
PANSY. Playing about behind my back under my very nose!

DICK. *You* know I've done all the dirty jobs ever since I came here.

BOTTLE. You've only been up the flues twice a day!

PANSY. *And* I made your hair stand on end first! That's gratitude for you!

DICK. I've no cause for gratitude to *you*. You put me in a wretched, leaking garret to sleep, and if it were not for my cat I'd be overrun with rats and mice. I shouldn't have a thing left!

BOTTLE (*to Pansy*) *Well!* Did you hear *that?*

PANSY. He's lying in his teeth. There isn't a rat or mouse in miles.

(SUKIE *enters, bearing a large rat in her mouth and one in each front paw. She goes to* PANSY, *who backs away, screaming*)

DICK. Bravo, Sukie! (*To Bottle*) See what I mean?

BOTTLE. That perishin' puss!

PANSY. Take it away! I've got one of me turns comin' on!

(PANSY *continues to back away, clutching her heart dramatically.* SUKIE *pursues her mischievously and* DICK *laughs.* PANSY *shrieks hysterically.*

ALICE *comes running in*)

ALICE. What is going on? (*She stops as she sees Pansy and Sukie*) Oh! What has Sukie got?

DICK (*going to her protectively*) Don't be afraid, Miss Alice. Sukie has been catching rats in my room.

ALICE. In *your* room? Oh, *no!*

DICK. And I'm afraid he was teasing Cook with the— er . . . (*He points to the rats*)

PANSY (*gasping*) He'll be my death! Me constitootion's too delicate . . .

BOTTLE. Yes, our Pansy's such a frail little flower.

(PANSY *simpers*)

DICK. Take those bodies away, Sukie!

(SUKIE *runs off* R, *very pleased*)

(*To Alice*) I'm sorry, Miss Alice.

ALICE. You've no need to apologize, Dick.
DICK. I must—er—get back to work. (*He moves to the exit*)
ALICE (*about to check him*) I...
BOTTLE. Ch'rm!
PANSY. Ahem!
(ALICE *checks herself and turns to them.*
DICK *exits* R)
ALICE. How dare you give that lad a rat-infested room! Give him another immediately! If you can't treat him decently you can both take a month's notice.
BOTTLE. What—*again?*
ALICE. This time I mean it. I'm determined to put a stop to this bullying.

(*The voices of* FITZWARREN *and* PERCY *are heard talking as they approach off* L)

(*Looking off* L) Oh, now there's that dreadful Percy Pilbeam coming. This is going to be an *awful* day! But remember what I said!

(ALICE *exits.* BOTTLE *and* PANSY *chortle with glee, slapping each other with delight. The voices come nearer*)

PANSY. Look out!

(*They straighten up.*
FITZWARREN *enters* L, *with* PERCY PILBEAM. PERCY *is a dandified, vacuous youth who carries a quizzing-glass which he uses frequently. He is inclined to turn his* "*r's*" *into* "*w's*")

FITZWARREN (*as they enter*) So you see, my dear fellow, I've thought it all out.
PERCY. Oh, quite so, quite so. Vastly entertaining—I mean interesting—I mean—most excellent, I'm sure.
FITZWARREN (*to Bottle*) Well, Bottle? And what are you doing in the warehouse?
BOTTLE. The parlour-maids, sir, were in here with the clerks. It's not right—I told them so.
FITZWARREN. Quite right. Most important!

PANSY. The new scullion was here, too, sir, a-gossiping with Miss Alice, I'm sorry to say. I told her she should remember his lowly station.
FITZWARREN. That, too, is important. We are all important in our way, eh, Pilbeam?
PERCY. Oh, *rather*, sir! My mother told me that I'm *fwightfully* important! I don't know why!
FITZWARREN. Whatever others may think, we must never forget——
BOTTLE. —our importance!
PANSY. How true!
FITZWARREN. Quite so! (*He surveys Bottle and Pansy coldly, and then turns to Percy as he commences the Number*)

No. 7. *Quartette*: "IMPORTANCE" (FITZWARREN, PERCY, BOTTLE and PANSY)
(Tune: *Lilliburlero*)

FITZWARREN.
    I am a merchant, Fitzwarren by name,
    Debit and Credit—Profit and Loss

(BOTTLE *and* PANSY *dance up stage, across and down*)

PERCY.
    I'd be the same, but oh, to my shame,
    Roll as a stone and gather no moss!

(FITZWARREN *and* PERCY *dance up stage, across and down, as* BOTTLE *and* PANSY *come down and sing*)

BOTTLE.
    I'm Bottle the Butler, I've wine in my eye!
PANSY.
    I'm Cook and there's none so important as I!

(ALL *down stage* C)

ALL (*pointing to each other*)
    You *may* be important,
    *He* may be important
    But none so important—

(*Each pointing to him or herself*)

    Important as *I!*

                    DANCE
FITZWARREN.
    My daughter will marry whomever I choose,
    Settlement—ring, honeymoon, font!
(BOTTLE *and* PANSY *dance up stage, across and down*)
PERCY.
    I fancy I'm booked to step in his shoes,
    'Twixt you and I, it's just what I want!
(FITZWARREN *and* PERCY *dance up stage, across and down, as* BOTTLE *and* PANSY *come down and sing*)
BOTTLE.  I'm Bottle, I buttle, and booze on the sly,
PANSY.
    I'm Pansy and none so important as I,
    (ALL *down stage* C)
ALL (*to her*)
    Did you say "important"?
PANSY.
    I *did* say "important"!
ALL (*each pointing to self*)
    There's none so important—important as *I!*
                    DANCE
BOTTLE.
    The "Quality" talk but dunno a lot!
    Sherry, Madeira, Brandy and Ale!
(FITZWARREN *and* PERCY *dance up stage, across and down as* BOTTLE *and* PANSY *sing*)
PANSY.
    If I told them all I've in the pot—
    Lummy, their tummies! They'd grow very pale!
(BOTTLE *and* PANSY *dance up stage as* FITZWARREN *and* PERCY *sing*)
FITZWARREN.  Fitzwarren, I!
PERCY.
    Here's "mud in your eye"!
    There's none so important . . .

FITZWARREN (*checking him*)
　Important as *I!*

(*A pause, while* FITZWARREN *and* PERCY *stare haughtily out front, and* BOTTLE *and* PANSY *walk down together to* RC, *and regard them for a moment or two in silence, before looking at each other*)

BOTTLE (*spoken*)
　Did they say *important?*
PANSY (*spoken; with a sniff*)
　They *did* say "important"!
ALL (*singing*)
　There's none so important—important as I!

(DANCE, *and exit,* BOTTLE *and* PANSY R, FITZWARREN *and* PERCY L.
　PERCY *re-enters* L *immediately.*
　ALICE *enters* R. *They meet* C, *and check*)

PERCY. Ah, good morning, Miss Alice!
ALICE. Good morning, Mr Pilbeam. (*Trying to pass him*) Excuse me, won't you—I'm very busy.
PERCY (*barring her way*) But I wanted to *talk* to you!
ALICE. What about?
PERCY (*giggling*) L-l-love!
ALICE (*startled*) Love? Couldn't we talk about the weather instead?
PERCY. No—let's stick to *love!*
ALICE. I don't know what you mean.
PERCY. Oh, *you* know! The stuff they croon about. (*He "croons" a few bars of a love song, very burlesqued*)

(ALICE *shudders*)

ALICE. And what do those bleats and moans mean?
PERCY. I love you!
ALICE. Oh, really. Very nice, I'm sure.
PERCY (*with a giggle*) And there's another thing—I want you to call me Percy and-and-and I want me to call you "Alice". Do you think me would let me—I mean you would let me?
ALICE. You can call me anything you like if only

## Scene 3   DICK WHITTINGTON

you'll let me get on with my household duties. (*Trying to pass*) Excuse me . . .
PERCY. Oh, I say, couldn't you get a bit more—you know—*enthusiasm* into it?
ALICE (*retreating a pace*) No, I could *not!*
PERCY. But your father told me he'd arranged that you *would!*
ALICE. Would what?
PERCY. Be enthusiastic—and—and marry me!

(ALICE *bursts into a peal of laughter*)

(*Going to her*) Oh, Alice—I really do love you—*enormously* . . .

(PERCY *seizes* ALICE *in his arms and kisses her. She pushes him away and boxes his ears.*
DICK *enters* R. PERCY *retreats a pace, holding his ear*)

DICK. Is there anything I can do for you, Miss Alice?
ALICE (*pretending to be haughty*) Yes, scullion! Show this fellow to the door! (*She winks at Dick, aside*)

(DICK *moves towards Percy*)

PERCY. I will not be shown the door by a scullion! (*He moves* L) I shall go and find a footman! *He'll* do it for me. (*Turning at the exit*) "Footman!" I shall say, "show me the door—at *once!*"

(PERCY *marches off in high dudgeon.*
ALICE *and* DICK *look at each other and laugh*)

ALICE. Poor Percy! (*Glancing down, mock demure*) Did you think I needed rescuing, sir?
DICK. I did! Was I *very* presumptuous?
ALICE (*demurely*) You were very *timely!* I am glad you were—near at hand.
DICK. I wish . . . (*He hesitates*)
ALICE. What do you wish?
DICK. I wish I could always be—near you. I wish I was rich, and famous, and that I could do all I long to do!
ALICE. What is it you wish to do so much?

DICK. I'm only a poor country boy. I've no right even to be speaking like this to the daughter of a rich merchant . . .

ALICE. Nonsense! I'm your friend. And I believe you *will* do great things one day, and the citizens of London will be proud to own you!

DICK. You really mean that? You give me fresh courage, and hope, Miss Alice . . . (*He breaks off, embarrassed*)

ALICE. Dick—when we're alone, couldn't you—drop the "Miss"?

DICK (*in wonder*) I may call you "Alice"?

(ALICE *nods*)

ALICE. Why not?

DICK. Always I feel you are my guardian angel. That night, when I opened my eyes and saw you above me, beautiful and compassionate—(*he turns away*)— I loved you.

ALICE (*softly*) Oh—Dick . . .

No. 8 *Duet* (ALICE *and* DICK)
(*After the Number,* ALICE *and* DICK *embrace.*
BOTTLE *enters* R)

BOTTLE (*checking and staring*) *Well!*

(ALICE *and* DICK *break apart*)

ALICE. You here *again*, Bottle?

BOTTLE. Indeed thus! And well is it that be so I should! And what do I behold? *Fun*—if not, as a further diversion—*games!*

ALICE. How dare you!

DICK. You've no right to speak to your mistress like that!

BOTTLE. And you've no right to answer me back, you young toad-in-the-turf, you lizard in the lettuce bed! You are dismissed. (*He whirls both arms wildly and nearly topples over*)

ALICE. Take no notice, Dick—he is not himself.

BOTTLE. Then who am I? Tell me that! Moreover, I caught you coyly kissing this petty potato peeler . . .
ALICE. That is none of your business, Bottle.
BOTTLE. It *is* my bottle, Business, bust me buttons! I shall report this carrot-scraping scullion. (*He holds up his hand*) Not a word! It is my duty, and I have a taste for duty!
DICK. I notice you have a lot of tasting duty in the wine cellar.
ALICE. If you say one word to father I shall report you for disobeying him and treating Dick so . . .
BOTTLE. I never treat no-one! I can't afford it!

(FITZWARREN *enters* L)

FITZWARREN. Is anything wrong, Alice? Mr Pilbeam has just gone home looking like a thunder cloud.
BOTTLE (*slyly*) A—haaaaaah! (*He grins*)
FITZWARREN. Any observations, Bottle?

(BOTTLE *catches* ALICE'S *warning eye*)

BOTTLE. No, sir. I've done all the observating necessary for the moment!

(BOTTLE *gives Alice an unpleasant smile and exits self-righteously*, R)

FITZWARREN (*to Dick; not very cordially*) Well, boy?
ALICE. Father, couldn't you give Dick a start in the warehouse? He wants to get on—he wants to be a merchant one day—like you.
FITZWARREN. H'm! Ambitions, eh? Well, we might try, if Cook gives him a good reference.
ALICE (*with a little show of dignity*) *I* give him a good reference, Father.
FITZWARREN (*a little grimly*) I've no doubt, my dear. In the meantime, young man, go and help the men shift those bales of silk in the yard.
DICK (*eagerly*) Yes, sir!

(DICK *runs off* R)

FITZWARREN. And now, my dear, I want to have a little word with *you*.

ALICE (*mock demurely; with a little curtsy*) Yes, Papa!

(ALICE *trips off down* L, *with demure little steps*. FITZWARREN *watches her go*)

FITZWARREN (*striding* L) Yes—*poppet!*

(FITZWARREN *exits down* L.

*The* CLERKS, *led by* FREDERICK, *enter up* L. *The* MAIDS, *led by* KITTY, *enter up* R. *They dance in to* "*Spring Song*" *and group, with* FREDERICK *and* KITTY *down* C. *Then they sing a reprise of the refrain of No.* 6 *to the same air as before*)

No. 8a *Reprise of No.* 6 (FREDERICK, KITTY, CLERKS *and* MAIDS)

FREDERICK.
 That's all for today—
 We must strive for higher pay—
ALL MEN.
 So to guard against all risk of derision—
KITTY (*singing on an ascending scale*) De-ri-hi-hi-hision
ALL (*slowly and deliberately*)
 With our melancholic flair
 For a Mendelssohnic air,
 We'll dance the "Fruhlingslied" with precision!
*They resume dancing to* "*Spring Song*".

*The* TABS *close after the first eight or ten bars, but the* MUSIC *continues as the Interlude Cloth is set*


SCENE 4

SCENE—*On the Road* (*Front Cloth*)
 *At* RC *is a milestone.*
 DICK *and* SUKIE *enter* R. DICK *carries a bundle on a stick over his shoulder. The music of the last Number continues softly until* DICK *seats himself on the milestone, with* SUKIE *beside him, then fades.*

DICK. We've come a long way since dawn, Sukie, haven't we?

(SUKIE *droops*)

Tired? So am I, old friend, but we must go on and put as many miles between us and Alderman Fitzwarren's house as possible before tonight.

(SUKIE *looks up at him pleadingly*)

No, we *can't* go back, Sukie. It's better for us to leave than to cause trouble.

(SUKIE *shakes her head stubbornly*)

Oh, yes, it is! Pansy and Bottle hate us—but it's for Alice's sake mostly we have to go. We can't be the cause of unhappiness between her and her father—and we should, if Bottle betrayed us.

(SUKIE *miaouws fiercely.* DICK *laughs in spite of himself*)

Yes, that's how *I* feel, too! (*He strokes Sukie*) I couldn't help falling in love with her, could I?

(SUKIE *shakes her head*)

Though I had no right to!

(SUKIE *nods violently and miaouws*)

Good old Sukie! It's true, though. So—back to the village, and good-bye dreams. (*His head droops over his knees*)

(SUKIE *droops. There is a pause. Then the* LIGHTS *rise very slowly as Bow Bells are heard very softly in the distance. It is a moment or two before* DICK *seems to hear them. Then he lifts his head slowly, and listens. The bells become a little louder, and* DICK *becomes more alert.* SUKIE *raises her head, too*)

Do you hear that, Sukie? Bow Bells! (*He rises*)
CHORUS (*off; singing*)
  Turn again, Whittington,
  Thrice Lord Mayor of London!

DICK. Do you hear? "Turn again, Whittington—*turn again!*" The message of Bow Bells, telling me to go back! "Thrice Lord Mayor of London!" Oh, Sukie—d'you think it's true?

(SUKIE *nods*)

You do? Then so do. I! I'm going back! Only a coward would run away! I'll fight my way up the ladder yet and win my Alice for a bride! Back, Sukie! If we hurry they'll never know we've been away! Back! And make the message of the bells come true! (*He sings*)

No. 9 *Song* "*Bow Bells*" (DICK)
(Tune: *The Bells of Aberdovey*)

Hark! The sound of old Bow Bells
Joyfully their ringing tells,
Courage take, and turn again
To be thrice Lord Mayor of London.
Ring out, ring out, bells of Bow,
And tell it out that all may know,
Dick Whittington's returning!

CHORUS (*off; singing*)

2

Citizens of London Town
Your fame you're ever prizing,
Hail a name to bring renown,
A worthy son is rising!
Hear the message of the bells,
Hear the news the chime foretells!
Turn again, Dick Whittington
To be thrice Lord Mayor of London!

DICK *joins in a reprise of the last refrain, then, as Bow Bells ring out triumphantly, he shoulders his pack, and with* SUKIE *at his side, he marches off* R.

CURTAIN

## ACT II

### Scene 1

SCENE—*Fitzwarren's Warehouse.*
*Some bales of material are set about, with lengths of silk, or other material displayed.*

*When the* CURTAIN *rises, the stage is filled with* MERCHANTS, *their* WIVES *and other* LADIES. *They are moving about and giving the impression of chatting together as they sing an opening Number. There is a good deal of business of examining and admiring the materials, etc., displayed.*

No. 10 *Ensemble* (MERCHANTS *and* LADIES)

(*Towards the end of the Number,* FITZWARREN *enters with* PERCY. *They move about among the company, exchanging greetings, etc.* PERCY *is in a flirtatious mood.* FITZWARREN *is very genial. After the Number, during miming of general conversation*)

1ST LADY. Oh, lovely! This brocade—gorgeous!
2ND LADY. My dear—a dream!
A MERCHANT. You think it will sell among my customers?
3RD LADY. My dear Henry—you should buy miles of it!
4TH LADY. The women will positively fight to get it.
MERCHANT (*to Fitzwarren*) What can I say, Fitzwarren? My wife is determined I shall ruin myself in speculation.
FITZWARREN. You need have no fear. The display is attractive, ladies? You owe it to my new under-manager—Master Richard Whittington, who is full of these artistic ideas!
1ST LADY. You mean the young man in brown I saw talking to your daughter in the courtyard? Such a handsome lad!

FITZWARREN (*a little brusquely*) He is not ill-looking, I think. Certainly he has converted the courtyard into a positive garden with his display of fabrics—for your pleasure, ladies. (*He bows*)

PERCY. The ladies—bless 'em all!

2ND LADY. But surely there's only one little lady for you, Mr Pilbeam?

PERCY. Oh, positively only one—at a time! (*He goes into a high-pitched peal of laughter*)

(*The general movement and business continues as* FITZWARREN *draws* PERCY *down stage*)

FITZWARREN (*to Percy*) I want you to be a little more serious, Pilbeam. Your father still shares my hope that the two most important merchant families in the City may be united by marriage before long. (*He pats Percy on the back*) You—and Alice.

PERCY. Oh, *rather*—I hadn't forgotten! But that fellow Whittington is always with her when I try to get a moment's conversation . . .

FITZWARREN. Whittington?

PERCY (*plaintively*) Positively! Impudent fellah!

FITZWARREN. I'll look into it! In the meantime, you have my permission to pay your addresses to my daughter.

PERCY. Oh, I don't mind what I *pay!*

FITZWARREN (*coldly*) Just your addresses.

PERCY. Twenty-eight Cotton Court, ninety-two Wilton Square . . .

FITZWARREN (*interrupting him; wearily*) Don't bother. Another time. Business first.

(DICK *enters* L. *He is dressed smartly in business clothes and carries some papers*)

Well, Whittington?

DICK. Some visitors, sir! (*He laughs*) No less than two special messengers from the King of the Boko Islands.

FITZWARREN. The King of *Boko?*

(*The others all turn and listen*)

DICK. They tell me they have a business proposition for you, sir, as the most influential importing merchant in London.

(*There is an approving murmur from the Company*)

FITZWARREN. Well, well, I don't know—however, invite them to come in at once.

(DICK *bows and exits* L)

(*To the Company*) You may find this interesting—or perhaps, amusing, ladies and gentlemen.

(DICK *enters* L, *ushering in* PING *and* PONG)

PERCY. I don't know about *interesting*, but certainly amusing. (*He gives his high peal of laughter*)

(PING *and* PONG *stare at Percy, then at each other, then echo the peal of laughter, then stare at each other again, and both make a despairing gesture with their hands*)

FITZWARREN (*to them*) Gentlemen——
PING. Ping!
PONG. Pong!

(ALL *laugh, except Fitzwarren and Dick.* PING *and* PONG *stare at each other*)

FITZWARREN. —I understand you come from His Majesty the King of the Boko . . .
PING }
PONG } (*together*) *Banga-Banga!*

(*The* LADIES *scream.* PING *and* PONG *roar with laughter—their laugh should start with a high shriek and then go very low*)

FITZWARREN. We shall be very pleased to do business with His Majesty . . .
PING }
PONG } (*together*) *Wallah-Wallah!*

FITZWARREN. Exactly—that is understood. You shall see our samples in the courtyard, but first of all we should like to entertain you.

PING  
PONG } (*together*)  No-no-no-no-*no!*  
FITZWARREN. I don't understand?  
PING. Dat is right—you don't understand—so!  
PONG. We sing you Boko song—very intelligent!  
PING. Do Boko dance—mos' intellectual!  
PONG. Here you have nothing like it!  
PING. Only in Boko is people so brainy to make it—yass!  
PONG. Yas*sah!*  
PING. Ho!  
PONG. Ko!  

No. 11  Duet, "THE BOKO SONG" *with Dance* (PING, PONG *and* COMPANY)  
(Air: *Ben Backstay*)  

(*During the Number* DICK *and* FITZWARREN *confer privately down* R. PERCY *and the rest watch and listen. They unconsciously imitate* PING *and* PONG'S *swaying and gestures, and join in the dance. Eventually the* CHORUS, *led by* PING *and* PONG *with* PERCY *between them, dance out* R, *leaving* FITZWARREN *and* DICK *alone*)

I
PING.  We come from Boko Islands  
      A spot right in de sun!  
PONG.  We're hotted up and roasted brown  
      But nevah, *nevah* done!  
PING.  No sah, we'm nevah done!  
BOTH.  We'm nevah, nevah *done!*  

CHORUS. For we come from Boko Land, jolly old Cocoa Land,  
      Singing merrily all the day long,  
      (*Dancing*) With a hop-hop-hoppity,  
      Jump and a-skippity,  
      Clip-clip-cloppity, dancing along!  
  (*Chorus repeated with* COMPANY)

SCENE 1     DICK WHITTINGTON     33

2
PONG. There ain't no deep depressions
No rain to soak us through.
PING. We never see an icicle
Or catch the Asian 'flu!
BOTH. No sah, we never pack
A brolley or a mack.!
(*Repeat Chorus as before*)

3
PING. We like-um you in London,
PONG. Oh yass! We see your sights!
PING. The soldiers marching up and down
PONG. We wait to see-um fights!
BOTH. But, boy, oh, boy! The gals—
We love the pretty gals!
(*Repeat Chorus as before.*
DICK *looks through his papers*)

FITZWARREN (*to Dick*) H'm I think this may be a chance to show that the name of Fitzwarren is really known all over the world. Now, I'll look after the display in the courtyard while you go and tell Alice to have tea served there at once—no! Here are Frederick and Kitty—they can see to it.

DICK. Very well, sir.

(FREDERICK *and* KITTY *enter* L)

FITZWARREN. Frederick, tell Miss Alice that tea must be served to the company in the courtyard as soon as possible. You help her, Kitty. (*To Dick*) Come with me, Whittington. The display is very good—I want you to give every attention to *business*.

(FITZWARREN *and* DICK *cross and exit* R)

FREDERICK. Well, now that they're out of the way . . . (*He seizes Kitty and kisses her*)

KITTY (*pushing him away*) You *are* a bad lad!

FREDERICK. I shouldn't be a bad lad if a bad girl didn't egg me on!

Kitty. Me? Bad? (*She moves* L) Good afternoon!
Frederick. Oh, Kitty, when I said "bad" I didn't mean "*bad*".
Kitty. Have you forgotten we have to tell Miss Alice that . . . (*She checks*) What *is* it we have to tell Miss Alice?
Frederick. Something about tea. (*He looks off* L) Oh, here are Bottle and Pansy—they'll do!

(Bottle *and* Pansy *enter* L)

Bottle. We'll do *what?*
Frederick. Anybody—I mean any*thing*—(*aside*) for money.
Kitty (*as if giving orders*) Mr Fitzwarren wishes tea served in the courtyard for everyone, including two little nigger boys. (*She waves them away*)
Pansy. Nigger boys? I pack my bag at once!

(Pansy *turns and marches off* L)

Bottle. Serve *tea?* I wouldn't demean meself!

(Bottle *marches off* L.
Frederick *and* Kitty *look at each other, shrug their shoulders and throw their arms wide in hopeless gestures*)

Kitty. No tea!
Frederick. Who cares?

No. 12 *Duet* (Frederick *and* Kitty)

(*The Number continues with a dance. At the end* Frederick *kisses Kitty and holds her at arm's length*)

Frederick. The prettiest little bit of goods in the warehouse!
Kitty. Who are *you* calling a little bit of goods, may I ask?
Frederick. Frederick Filer, chief folio filler to Fitzwarren's, and your future food-finder!
Kitty. Oh, Freddy!

(Kitty *throws herself into Frederick's arms, gives him a quick embrace and the dance is resumed. It is interrupted after about six bars by the hurried re-entrance of* DICK, R. *They break apart guiltily*)

DICK (*checking* RC) Frederick! Kitty! Where is that tea?

FREDERICK. Tea, sir?

KITTY. Tea?

DICK (*angrily*) Yes—*tea!*

(ALICE *enters* L)

ALICE. It's all right, Mr Whittington. Pansy has made it and Bottle is serving it!

(*The others gasp and stare open-mouthed*)

DICK. How did you manage that?

ALICE (*primly*) One only needs to be *firm*, Mr Whittington, and one can get *anything*.

DICK. Frederick, assist Mr Fitzwarren in the courtyard.

ALICE. Kitty, assist Pansy in the pantry.

(FREDERICK *and* KITTY *turn* R *and* L *respectively, and exit*)

DICK (*going to her*) Alice . . .

ALICE. Really, Mr Whittington! And what may you be wanting?

DICK. You! Mr Pilbeam or no Mr Pilbeam, I—want —*you!*

ALICE. Indeed!

DICK. Yes, and one only needs to be *firm*, Miss Fitzwarren, and one can get *anything!*

ALICE. So I'm an "anything"?

DICK. You're *everything*—to *me!*

No. 13 *Duet* (ALICE *and* DICK)

(*At the end of the Number, they are about to approach each other, but check as* FITZWARREN *enters* R)

FITZWARREN (*coming to* RC; *after a momentary pause*) Alice, my dear, you are neglecting your duties. The ladies—tea . . .

ALICE (*with a prim little curtsy; demurely*) Yes, Papa!

(ALICE *trips across and exits* R. FITZWARREN *watches her go, then turns to Dick*)

FITZWARREN (*rather coldly*) H'm—Whittington, I was wondering where you had got to. There's big business afoot, I think. This King of the Boko Islands is very keen to trade with us. He has ivory, precious stones, and rare timber to barter.

DICK. A wonderful opportunity, sir.

FITZWARREN. Of which we must take advantage at once. I propose to send out an expedition to the Boko Islands of which you, Whittington, will be in sole charge.

DICK. I, sir?

FITZWARREN. You. I—um—(*after a glance off* R) I particularly want *you* to go—to further my plans for the future. I shall charter a ship tomorrow. You will be away about a year.

DICK (*trying to hide his dismay*) A *year?* But—I may take my cat, sir?

FITZWARREN. Of course, of course!

(*Music of No.* 11 *is heard off* R.
FREDERICK *re-enters* R)

What is it, Frederick?

FREDERICK. The merchants, sir, are waiting to take their leave. Those Boko Islanders do nothing but dance!

FITZWARREN. Well, dance 'em all in here!

(FREDERICK *runs off* R. FITZWARREN *turns to Dick*)

Ah, Whittington, it'll make a stir in the City when I tell these people what's afoot!

DICK (*moving down* L) Yes, sir. (*He stands, turned away, disconsolate*)

(*The* CHORUS, *led by* PING *and* PONG, *with* PERCY *between them, dance in* R, *singing the refrain of No.* 11. ALICE *enters last, and stands down* R. *Having filled the stage,* FITZWARREN *stops them, raising his hand*)

FITZWARREN (*up* LC) Ladies and gentlemen! Mr

## SCENE 1     DICK WHITTINGTON

Pilbeam, perhaps you will give my daughter the pleasure of your attendance.

PERCY (*leaving Ping and Pong*) Oh, positively!

ALICE (*as if she has not heard this; crossing quickly to Dick*) Dick! What is this I hear?

(PERCY *and* FITZWARREN *stare at them, reacting*)

FITZWARREN. Ladies and gentlemen! You will, I know, be delighted to hear that our City has been honoured by the opening of trade between my company and no less than His Majesty the King of the Boko Islands!

(*Cheers.* BOTTLE *and* PANSY *enter* L, *and listen*)

PING } (*together*) Ho! Ko! Wallah! Wallah! Chah!
PONG

FITZWARREN. Thank you very much.

PING } (*together*) *Ko!*
PONG

FITZWARREN. Naturally! An expedition will sail next week, and I am putting my new under-manager, Mr Richard Whittington, in full charge of the whole affair!

(*Cheers*)

It will take at least a year.

ALICE. Papa, don't you think *Mr Pilbeam* would be more suitable?

PERCY. Oh, positively *not!* A year! What would London do without me? And what should *I* do without London? Oh, positively *not!*

FITZWARREN. My party will have every comfort. Bottle will be ship's steward, and Pansy will be cook.

PANSY. Cook? Never! I pack my bags!

(PANSY *marches off* L)

BOTTLE. Steward? Wouldn't demean meself.

(BOTTLE *marches off* L)

PERCY. In the meantime, I'm all for Whittington wandering west! Let's give him a rousing send-off!

ALL. Hurrah!

(ALL *group and sing*)

No. 14 *Ensemble* (The COMPANY)

*As the Number starts,* FITZWARREN *goes down to Alice, takes her hand, and leads her down* R. *In the meantime,* PERCY *has danced from down* R *to* C, *joining* PING, PONG *and four of the* LADIES. *It is not until* FITZWARREN *reaches down* R *that he finds Percy is not there. He reacts angrily on seeing what has happened. As the Number proceeds,* ALICE *down* R, *and* DICK *down* L, *look at each other. Finding* FITZWARREN *is watching them both, they turn away until the Number comes to an end and—*
    *the* TABS *close*

INTERLUDE. *In Front of* TABS *during scene change.*
*A sea chest has been pushed on stage* L. DICK *enters* L. *He carries a length of thin rope, and is followed by* SUKIE.

DICK. Come on, Sukie. There's nothing for it—we've got to go, so let's rope up the chest and make the best of it.

(SUKIE *jumps on to the chest*)

Hey! Wait a minute! Let's see if we have everything.

(SUKIE *jumps off the chest, and* DICK *opens it and looks inside*)

Yes, spare boots, four shirts, storm jacket, hair brush. Hey! What's this? (*They both peer into the chest.* DICK *takes out a small picture set into a folding case. He opens it*) Alice! A miniature portrait of my Alice! She must have put it there this morning, after I'd packed. (*He kisses the picture*)

(SUKIE *miaouws*)

Want to have a look? There you are! (*He shows Sukie the picture*)

(SUKIE *miaouws with approval*)

Of course it's a good likeness! It's perfect! How good of

her—it must mean that she cares for me in spite of everything.

(ALICE *enters* R)

(*Not having seen Alice*) Let's put it back safely, between the new shirts. (*He packs the picture*) It can't break now. (*As he ropes the chest*) Her picture! It must mean she cares!

(SUKIE *miaouws*)

It'll be awful away from her, Sukie. You'll have to comfort me as much as you can. (*He tugs at the rope*) I'll give you as good a time as I can, Sukie. (*He ties the last knot*) But it'll be pretty grim without Alice—I love her so.

ALICE (*gently*) I'm glad.

DICK (*turning, and springing to his feet*) Alice! Oh, thank you, thank you!

ALICE (*smiling*) You like it?

DICK. Only one thing could I want more—your love.

ALICE. You have that, too.

DICK. And you have mine, if you want it. You are my inspiration! I shall think of you night and day and dream of our next meeting.

ALICE. It is so long to wait.

DICK. You're sure you want to wait? (*Mischievously*) There's always Pilbeam!

ALICE (*laughing*) How absurd you are! You've nothing to fear from him!

DICK. But your father . . . ?

ALICE. We'll cross that bridge when we come to it.

DICK. I'll make this expedition a success, Alice! I'll make myself worthy to be his son-in-law . . .

ALICE. You're that already!

(SUKIE *miaouws*. ALICE *and* DICK *look at him and laugh*. SUKIE *settles down to sleep*)

No. 14a *Reprise of No.* 13 (DICK *and* ALICE)

*At the end of the Number the lights—*

BLACK-OUT

## Scene 2

Scene—*The deck of a ship.*
*This is played in front of a cloth, at half-stage depth, depicting the side of the ship and sky above.*

*The* Tabs *open on a darkened stage and sound of wind and distant thunder. This continues as the lighting rises slowly, and dies away as the* Sailors *enter* r *and* l, *singing a rollicking nautical number.*

### No. 15  *Chorus* (Sailors)

(*During the dance which follows,* Pansy *enters* l *and joins in, singing also the repeat refrain and joining in the repeat dance*)

Pansy (*gasping and mopping her brow*) Coo! Now I know what it feels like to be a scrambled egg!
1st Sailor. You're a game old bird, Ma!
Pansy. Old bird? Let me tell you in Wapping I'm considered very *chic!*
2nd Sailor. But this ain't Wapping!
Pansy. Would that it were!
Sailors. 'Ear! 'Ear!
Pansy. Any more sauce from you and you can cook your own grub!
Sailors. *Hooray!*

(*Wind and distant thunder is heard. The* Sailors *rock a little on their feet.* Pansy *staggers.*
Bottle *totters on* l, *holding his head and groaning*)

Bottle. Stop the boat! Ring the bell! I want to get out!

(*The* Sailors *are highly amused*)

Pansy. But it's dinner-time!

(Bottle *groans*)

Don't you want any of my nice fried rissoles?

## SCENE 2     DICK WHITTINGTON     41

BOTTLE. *No!*
PANSY. Do you feel like a nice fat chop?
BOTTLE. I feel like death!

(*The* SAILORS *groan derisively in unison*)

PANSY. There's gratitude for you! The trouble you were to stow away!

(BOTTLE *staggers as wind and thunder is repeated, and the lights dim*)

BOTTLE. Stow me away again! I'll be no trouble *at all!*

(*Wind, thunder and lightning*)

3RD SAILOR (*clapping* BOTTLE *on the back and making him totter*) Cheer up, mate! You're not dead yet!
BOTTLE. What a pity!

(BOTTLE *and* PANSY *clutch each other and stagger*)

4TH SAILOR. Long way to go, chum!

(*Wind and thunder*)

1ST SAILOR. Bit of a breeze, I think!
PANSY. You *think!*
2ND SAILOR. Might be a storm later.
BOTTLE. "Might be"!
PANSY. Yes, he's not *quite sure!*

(*Thunder—wind howls*)

BOTTLE. *I* am! (*He staggers up to the back-cloth and claws at the ship's rail painted on it, of course to no purpose. He turns and wails at Pansy*) I can't get a grip of *anything!*

(*Thunder.* BOTTLE *spins round and is caught by two* SAILORS *who plump him down on a coil of rope* R)

PANSY. Get a grip of yourself—like *me.*

(*Thunder.* PANSY *staggers and spins round and falls into the arms of* SAILORS *and throws them off indignantly.*

CAPTAIN BILGE *and* DICK *enter* L. *The Captain has a very hale and hearty manner and a bristling red beard*)

CAPTAIN. Ahoy, there!
PANSY. Ahoy yourself!
CAPTAIN. I don't know how! (*Calling aloft, a little louder*) Ahoy, there! Splice the jib! Bedizen the boom! And when it's bedizened, bedizen it again!
PANSY. Coo! Whatever faw-wer?
CAPTAIN. It takes their minds off things.
DICK. How many knots can we do, Captain?
CAPTAIN. Let me see—there's the granny knot, the reef knot, the *ought* not, the *rather* not—but it's so long since I was in the Scouts . . .
DICK. Have we rounded the Cape yet?
CAPTAIN. No, but we've squared the Pelisse!
PANSY. That must have cost you something!

(*Wind, thunder*)

DICK. Well, folk, it looks as if we shall have a stormy landing!
CAPTAIN. How right you are!
BOTTLE. I want to go home!
CAPTAIN. Sailors, batten these landlubbers down below amidships!
SAILORS (*ad lib. as they go to* PANSY *and* BOTTLE) Aye, aye, sir.
CAPTAIN. And when you've done that, you can batten me down as well.
SAILORS. Aye, aye, sir. (*They seize* PANSY *and* BOTTLE) Come on, Joyful! Come on, Ma! Down below!

(*Some* SAILORS *drag Bottle off* R)

PANSY (*as she moves* R *with the* SAILORS; *to the Captain*) Cheerio, old salt! See you at dinner!

(PANSY *exits with the rest of the* SAILORS, *who sing a shanty as they go*)

CAPTAIN (*to* DICK) Did she say "dinner"?

(DICK *nods*)

I thought it was *tea!*

(*Wind. The* CAPTAIN *lurches slightly and steadies himself by holding Dick's arm*)

Excuse me—don't tell anybody, but I'm not cut out for this sort of thing!
DICK. I love it! It makes me want to *sing!*
CAPTAIN. *Sing? I* want to burst—but not into song!

(DICK *and the* CAPTAIN *do some steps to the intro. music*)

No. 16 *Duet* "THE LIFE FOR ME" (DICK *and* CAPTAIN)
(Tune: *The Lincolnshire Poacher*—slightly adapted)

DICK.       I love the life on the rolling wave—
CAPTAIN. I hate the sight of the sea!
DICK.       Whenever I see a rolling wave—
CAPTAIN. I want to go home to tea!
DICK.       The more it rolls, the more I want—
CAPTAIN. To get right home to my tea!
DICK (*repeating above line*) To lead a life on the sea!
CAPTAIN (*sustained wail*)
            O-o-ow! A sailor's life is the life for *you*,
            But *not* the life for *me!*
DICK (*repeating above two lines*)
            Oh, a sailor's life is no life for *you,*
            But just the life for *me!*

(*They dance a few steps*)

CAPTAIN (*spoken mournfully*) Tantivvy, tantivvy, tantivvy! A-hunting we will go!
DICK. What's hunting got to do with it?
CAPTAIN. Nothing whatever. I just wanted to change the subject.
DICK. Let's try again.
CAPTAIN. *Must* we?
DICK. Of course!
CAPTAIN (*with resignation*) Carry on, shipmate.

2ND VERSE

DICK. I hope we meet with some pirates bold!
CAPTAIN. I hate the sight of they!
DICK. We'll board and lock 'em in the hold—
CAPTAIN. And then go home to tay—(*spoken*) I mean "*tea*".
DICK. Oh, can't you think of aught but tea?
CAPTAIN. There's nothing nicer *than!*
(*Repeating line*) For ay poor sailor man!
DICK. O-oh—a sword for me and a marlin-spike,
And you can have your tea!
CAPTAIN (*repeating the line*)
O-o-oh—you fight what battles and who you like,
If I can have my tea!

(*They dance a few steps*)

CAPTAIN (*spoken*) There's only one thing in the world more beautiful than daffodils.
DICK. And what's that?
CAPTAIN. Mazawattee. Mind you—the water must be really *boiling* . . .
DICK (*cutting in*) This is the last verse—the end of the song.
CAPTAIN. It'll be the end of me, too.

3RD VERSE

DICK. The sea gives *me* such an appetite . . .

(*Pause. The* CAPTAIN *goes* L, *and leans against the proscenium as he sings*)

CAPTAIN. I'm feeling most upset.
DICK. I do not like my meals too light—
CAPTAIN (*holding his stomach*)
My meals I can't forget!
DICK. The more I eat, the more I want,
CAPTAIN. I eat, and want to die!
DICK (*repeating line*)
I'd love a hot pork pie!

(*This line could be spoken, if desired*)

CAPTAIN. Ooow, you *are* unkind, for *now* I find
I don't want even *tea!* (*He regards Dick with disgust*)

DICK (*repeating above lines*)
O-oh, come storm and wind, I know I'll find
The sea's the life for *me!*

(DICK *does a little dance to a repeat of the last two or three lines, which takes him off* R, *while the* CAPTAIN *turns his eyes to heaven in disgust and despair*)

CAPTAIN (*spoken*) I shall report this to the Society for the Prevention of Cruelty to Sailors.

(DICK *re-enters* R)

DICK (*as he crosses to the Captain*) Well, what course are you on now, sir?

CAPTAIN. "Domestic Plumbing for the Handy Husband."

(DICK *looks puzzled*)

Oh, I see what you *mean!* Well, according to the second Mate's calculations, we're heading straight for Parson's Green! (*Or local town*)

DICK. Well, Parson's Green or the Boko Islands, what does it matter so long as it's dry land?

CAPTAIN. Bash me with a bowsprit! Don't tell me you're tired of this luxury cruise already!

DICK. Already? Why, we've been at sea three months and a rough passage all the way!

CAPTAIN (*airily*) Oh, it gets a bit choppy at times . . .

(*Sudden howl of wind. The* CAPTAIN *staggers and clutches Dick*)

Excuse me. (*He detaches himself and looks through a telescope*) We're getting near land!

DICK (*eagerly*) What can you see?

CAPTAIN. Nothing, but I can tell by the way me corns are shooting!

DICK. This is a great adventure for me! What, I wonder, will these islands be like? Rich—exotic—mysterious—full of strange——

CAPTAIN. —smells. And danger! You'll see things you've never seen before! Sea serpents that drag you down and crush your bones—quite a sensation! Dragons breathing fire—ruins the ice-cream! Black men cooking missionaries! Chocolate girls selling pea-nuts! Flying fish on frying nights! Elephants playing book-ends—crocodiles weeping over handbags that were once in the family!

DICK (*enthralled*) It's fantastic!

CAPTAIN. Aye, you'll love it—*if* you can escape the man-eating spider! What appetites! Does you good to watch them.

(*A bell sounds*)

And speaking of watches, that's the third watch—I must go and wind it! (*He goes* L *and turns*) Don't let what I've said *worry* you!

(*The* CAPTAIN *exits* L)

DICK. Sailor's yarns! Well, they add spice to the adventure! How I wish I had Alice here to share it with me.

(SUKIE *enters* R, DICK *turns to see him*)

Hullo, Sukie! Come to cheer me up? You're a wonderful pal! (*He strokes the cat*) I'm never half so lonely when you're around! (*He sings*)

No. 16a (DICK)

(*This should be a short reprise of No. 13*)

(PANSY *enters* R, *pushing* BOTTLE *before her. He is tottering and staggering*)

PANSY. There you are! (*She gives him a push up stage*) Drape yourself over the rail.

(BOTTLE claws *at the painted rail on the cloth*)

BOTTLE. I still can't get it!
PANSY (*exasperated*) Well, *pretend* you can!

(SUKIE *spits, miaouws, and gives Dick a comic nudge. Both laugh.* BOTTLE *stands like a question-mark, knees sagging, bowed shoulders, hands hanging down.* SUKIE *dances down* R, *and sits watching*)

DICK (*to Bottle*) What's the matter now? You were ordered below.
PANSY. We couldn't stand being shut up like sardines.
BOTTLE (*wailing*) Not *sardines!*
PANSY. Well, soused herrings then.

(BOTTLE *moans and sways*)

DICK. He should never have come.
PANSY. He needed a pick-me-up! Ozone! Sniff it!

(DICK *and* SUKIE *do a long "Bisto" sniff.* BOTTLE *howls. The* CAPTAIN *rushes in* L, *followed by the* SAILORS)

CAPTAIN. Land ahoy! All change!
DICK. Hooray! (*He takes the Captain's telescope from him and looks through it*)
PANSY. Where are we?

(BOTTLE *comes down. All look out front*)

CAPTAIN. Latitude twelve, longitude two thousand five hundred and seventy-eight nor' nor' east and then a little port.
PANSY. Port? I never touch it!
DICK (*taking the telescope from his eye*) I can see land—and a canoe coming this way and two small figures paddling! (*He looks through the telescope again*)
PANSY. A canoe?
CAPTAIN (*shouting*) Number Seventeen—come in! Your time's up! (*He titters*) Thought I was back at Blackpool! (*Or other seaside resort*)
BOTTLE. We going to land in a canoe?
PANSY. I can't get all *me* in *that!*
DICK. It's Ping and Pong!
CAPTAIN. Sailors, help them aboard!

1ST and 2ND SAILORS. Aye, aye, sir!

(*The two* SAILORS *run off* L)

CAPTAIN. Sailors! Have you your copies of the Song of Welcome?

SAILORS. *Aye, aye, sir!*

(*The* SAILORS *whip out copies of music*)

CAPTAIN. I'll give you a note. (*He takes out a huge tuning-fork*)

PANSY. Make it a fiver!

(*The* CAPTAIN *strikes the deck with the fork. A loud wailing "ping" is heard*)

CAPTAIN (*singing a high note*) Doh!

(*The* SAILORS *stand like a village glee party, assume absurdly earnest expressions and commence to chant "Song of the Volga Boatmen" to "Oh" and "Ah", etc.* PANSY *and* BOTTLE *weep on each other's shoulders. The* CAPTAIN *bursts into tears and mops his eyes with a red handkerchief.* DICK *is bewildered and highly amused. Loud cheers off* L)

DICK. Here they are!

(*The two* SAILORS *re-enter* L)

1ST SAILOR. Two messengers to see you, Cap'n!

2ND SAILOR. Werry urgent, Cap'n!

CAPTAIN. What do they want? If it's the instalment on the new binnacle, they're unlucky. This is the week for the telly.

(PING *and* PONG, *dressed exotically with feathers in their head-dress, shields and spears, rush in* L, *push aside the Sailors, nearly knock the Captain over, and make for Dick,* PANSY *clutches* BOTTLE, *who pushes her in front and hides behind her*)

PANSY (*throwing up her hands*) Pax! I'm not playing!

DICK (*shaking hands with Pong*) Ping!

PONG. Pong!

DICK (*shaking hands with Ping*) Pong!

PING. Ping!
CAPTAIN. Ping? Pong? Any relation to the Badmintons?
DICK. They come from King Banga-Banga of the Boko Islands!
PING. *Ho!*
PONG. *Ko!* Do much business with Massa Dickum Wittumtum!
DICK. They're very friendly!
CAPTAIN. Never can tell! The last trader who came here sold them *pressure cookers!*
PANSY. I knew it!
BOTTLE. Cannibals!
PING. We hope you not be too tough to us!
PONG. King Banga-Banga want you all for dinner tonight!
PANSY (*starting to go* R) I'm packing my bags this instant!
BOTTLE (*going to follow*) I'm out in sympathy!

(PING *and* PONG *have taken out small saucepans and metal ladles, and pretend to tune them up like instruments*)

DICK. Stop! It's an invitation!
PANSY. Oh, *is* it!
CAPTAIN. I think you may take what they say with a grain of salt.
PANSY. Well, so long as they don't take *me* with a grain of salt, I don't mind!
PING (*to Bottle*) Massa Bottle my best friend! (*He gives Bottle his spear and shield*)
PONG. Miss Pansy my pin-up gal—ho *yass!* (*He gives Pansy his spear and shield*)

(PANSY *and* BOTTLE *are speechless, with spears and shields*)

DICK. My friends, the long voyage is over! Tonight we banquet with King Banga-Banga, and his Queen!
PING }
PONG } (*together*) *Ho ko!*
SAILORS. Hooray!

DICK. Tomorrow we begin a new task of expanding—

(*A loud sharp bang is heard*)

PANSY (*clutching her waist*) Another button gone!
DICK. —trade in the Bokos! Let's greet our new friends with a song!
SAILORS. Aye, aye!
CAPTAIN. Shall I give you "doh"?

(*He bangs the tuning-fork and sings a note in a different key.* ALL *cheer and re-group as they sing*)

No. 17   *Ensemble* (*The* COMPANY)

*The* TABS *close*

INTERLUDE. *In Front of* TABS *during scene change*

No. 18   *Song* (ALICE)

(*This should be a nostalgic Number*)

## SCENE 3

SCENE—*The Boko Islands.*

*The scene is set in King Banga-Banga's compound. A rough shelter is* RC, *wherein are two seats arranged as thrones. Background of palms and exotic vegetation. One or two logs or rough stools* R *and* L. *The whole set should be very primitive.*

*When the* CURTAIN *rises, two* NATIVES *are standing up* R *and* L *respectively, holding large palm-leaf fans. Music. A crowd of* NATIVES *rush on, yelling and dancing. They fill the stage and then postrate themselves in a wide circle. The* KING *and* QUEEN *enter and go around in procession while the* NATIVES *on their knees, make obeisances and utter cries. The* KING *and* QUEEN *are dressed in a peculiar, but highly colourful assortment of clothes. For example, the* KING *may wear a top-hat, a football jersey, and a kilt. The* QUEEN *may be equally grotesque, with an enormous feathered hat, of which*

she is very proud. *After circling the stage once, the* KING
*and* QUEEN *go* C *and sing.*

No. 19 *Duet, Chorus and Dance* (KING, QUEEN *and*
NATIVES)
(Air: *The Tailor and the Mouse*)

1

KING. I am the King of Boko Land!
CHORUS. Banga-banga-banga-banga!
QUEEN. *I* am the Queen—so gr-r-reat and gr-r-rand!
CHORUS. Clang-clanga-clanga-clanga!
CHORUS OF NATIVES (*all dancing wildly*)
    Wah, walla-walla! Hokum-pokum!
    Coconuts and spices,
    Hi diddle bonkum! Monkey up tree!
    Wow! For the rats and mices!

2

KING (*pompously*)
    Big Chief of all the tribes am I!
CHORUS. Bang-banga-banga-banga!
QUEEN (*simpering*)
    They call me Little Dragon-Fly!
CHORUS. Clang-clanga-clanga-clanga!

    (ALL *dancing wildly*)

    Wah, walla-walla! Rantrum-tantrum!
    Rice and tapioca,
    Boom diddy boom boom, kippers for tea!
    (*Pointing to the Queen*)
    Bone-in-the-throat and choke 'er!

3

KING. White man he come and bring much trade!
CHORUS. Bang-banga-banga-banga!
QUEEN (*very coy*)
    Betcha he'll call me "pretty maid"!
CHORUS. Clang-clanga-clanga-clanga!

    (ALL *dancing wildly*)

Wah, walla-walla, junkum-bunkum!
Peppercorns and jalop,
Ping tinga-linga, woollem-pullem,
Half a pint of wallop!

4

KING. We'll greet white man with Boko roar!
CHORUS (*yelling*)
Bang-banga-banga-banga!
QUEEN (*shouting*)
Let's make it rip from shore to shore!
CHORUS. Clang-clanga-clanga-clanga!

(ALL *dancing wildly*)

Wah, walla-walla, diddle-fiddle!
£. s. d. and dollars,
Rah, riddle-diddle, boggem-floggem,
Rah! For the wide-boy wallahs!

(ALL *dance. After the dance, the* KING *and* QUEEN *take their seats* RC)

KING (*clapping his hands*) Ho!
ALL. Ko!
KING (*to the attendant*) White man come?
ATTENDANT. White man come, massa.
QUEEN (*proudly*) White man like um hat. (*She adjusts the hat carefully*) Take-um me back London—yassah!
KING (*rubbing his hands*) Yass! White man welcome! Plenty trade—all rich men! Sellum diamonds, sellum Queen—good business!

(PING *and* PONG *enter* L *to native drums, followed by* CAPTAIN BILGE *and* DICK. PING *and* PONG *suddenly prostrate themselves before the King and Queen, and the* CAPTAIN *falls over them*)

CAPTAIN (*as he tries to rise*) Sorry to drop in on you like this!

(DICK *helps the* CAPTAIN *to his feet*)

(*To the King and Queen*) Well, old fruits! The Navy's here!

DICK (*bowing ceremonially*) We are deeply honoured by your Majesties' invitation.

(PING *and* PONG *rise and stand up* C)

KING (*to Ping*) What they mean?

PING. They say they tickled to bits, massa.

PONG. Yassah!

QUEEN (*very seductively; to the Captain*) You like-um hat?

CAPTAIN (*averting his eyes*) What a lid!

KING. Queen for sale! Lovely bargain!

(*The* NATIVES *murmur approval*)

DICK (*hastily*) Your Queen is indeed beautiful, your Majesty. We are overwhelmed!

(*The* QUEEN *simpers*)

CAPTAIN. Fair hit amidships!

QUEEN (*with a high-pitched giggle*) White men are so wonderful!

DICK. We bring greetings from Alderman Fitzwarren of London to your Majesties. We hope to trade with your people.

KING. Trade—*good!* Much trade tomorrow! To-night—banquet! You ready for eating?

DICK. Well, it depends what you mean!

QUEEN. Pot luck!

CAPTAIN (*aghast*) *Pot* luck? (*To Dick*) It's those pressure cookers!

KING (*clapping his hands*) Ping! Pong! Go—prepare big feast!

(DICK *and the* CAPTAIN *shake hands.*

PING *and* PONG *prostrate themselves and crawl out backwards* R)

DICK (*looking round*) So this is the Boko Islands! How beautiful it is! Perhaps I shall lay the foundation of my fortune here.

KING. You like um?
CAPTAIN. Beautiful!
QUEEN (*simpering and fluttering her eyelids at the Captain*) Gorgeous!

(*The* CAPTAIN *backs away, alarmed.*
PING *and* PONG *come rushing in* R, *chattering excitedly*)

PING. Rats! Rats!
PONG. Food—all gone!
PING. Rats—eat um all!
PONG. Drag um away!

(*The* KING *and* QUEEN *spring to their feet and howl with rage. The* NATIVES *chatter and gesticulate*)

KING (*pacing around*) My bee-yutiful feast!
QUEEN (*pacing around*) Rats! Aaaah! I swaint! I foon!

(*The* QUEEN *begins to fall into the* CAPTAIN's *arms but he dodges behind Dick*)

DICK. Oh, dear! Something's gone wrong!

(ALL *shout*)

ALL (*ad lib.*) Rats! Rats! It's rats—eat *us!*
KING. Dirty great rats! They plagues! We keep nothings—they take everythings!
QUEEN. Go bonkers!
CAPTAIN (*to Dick*) Trade 'em some traps.
DICK. I can do better than that! Sukie! *She'll* deal with them! (*He bows to the King and Queen*) Leave it to me, and my cat, your Majesties!
KING. *Ho!*
QUEEN. *Ko!*

(*The* NATIVES *cheer.*
DICK *exits* L)

KING. No food, so bringum wine! We roastum Captain!

(*The* CAPTAIN *reacts*)

QUEEN. Toastum—no roastum!
KING. Bring wine! No roast—make-um toast!
CAPTAIN. Oh, *good!*
QUEEN. Wine!
KING. Girls!
QUEEN. Peanuts!
CAPTAIN. Programme!

(DANCING GIRLS *and* WINE BEARERS *enter and* ALL *go into a wild rock 'n roll dance with shouts and cries, and then, exit.*
PANSY *and* BOTTLE *enter* L, *looking about them curiously*)

PANSY. What a set-up! You'd think you was in my old Mum's parlour with all these pot plants about.
BOTTLE. It's not natural! I don't know where they get 'em from.
PANSY. There's a place in . . . Street—but we're asked not to advertise. (*Looking around*) Hasn't everything got a funny look about it?
BOTTLE (*significantly*) *You* should talk! (*He moves about peering at everything*)
PANSY. I mean to! Where's His Nibs, Dick Whittington?
BOTTLE. You bet he's throwing his weight about as usual.
PANSY. Yes, thinks himself somebody! Doesn't know Fitzwarren sent him off to stop him hanging about Miss Alice!
BOTTLE (*sitting down under a palm tree*) Ha! By the time we get back she'll be Mrs Percy P-Pilbeam! That'll learn 'im!
PANSY. He'll lose face.
BOTTLE. That'll be no loss.
PANSY. Oh, I dunno. (*She sits on the King's chair*) He's not a bad lad.
BOTTLE. There you go! (*He mimics her*) "Not a bad lad!" Cor crown me with a coconut . . .

(*A coconut suddenly falls from above and lands on the stage close to* BOTTLE, *with a crash. He reacts and stares up to the sky*)

PANSY (*amused*) You wanna be careful what you say round here!

BOTTLE. Lummy—I wanna *sedative!*

PANSY (*rising and moving to* C) I'll sing to you.

BOTTLE. Don't see the connection.

PANSY (*yelling at him*) Something soothing!

BOTTLE. I 'eard.

No. 20 *Song* (PANSY)

(*This should be a very boisterous "Sophie Tucker" type of Number.*

*During the Number* BOTTLE *nods and dozes.* PING *and* PONG *enter in time to join in the last refrain.* BOTTLE *rouses and joins in a final Dance which takes them off* R.

DICK *enters* L, *with* SUKIE, *who has a dead rat in her jaws*)

DICK (*as they enter*) Well done, Sukie! You've made a good start with those rats. (*He stops* C *and turns to Sukie*) How many did you get?

(SUKIE *holds up her paws and opens and closes them to indicate about fifty*)

(*Laughing*) All that? (*Patting the cat*) Well, I don't know where you put 'em all! Thank goodness I brought you with me.

(SUKIE *nestles against him*)

Now you know what you have to do, don't you? Kill every rat on the island—it's overrun with them. They're destroying everything. Kill 'em all, Sukie, d'you hear?

(SUKIE *nods several times, spits and miaouws*)

There'll be a terrible famine if you don't. Kill the lot! Then the King will be so pleased that our fortune will be made. Alderman Fitzwarren's trade will be established, and—who knows—he may consent to my marriage to Alice!

(SUKIE *gives a loud miaouw. They both start to do a few steps, but they are interrupted by the* CAPTAIN *who rushes in* R, *pursued by the* QUEEN)

CAPTAIN. Help! Save me! (*He dodges behind Dick and Sukie*)

QUEEN. He be my dream!

CAPTAIN. She be my nightmare!

(DICK *stands in the* QUEEN'S *way*)

QUEEN. He be wun'ful! He be—he be—he be . . .

CAPTAIN. She's got the heebee-jeebees!

(SUKIE *jumps towards the* QUEEN, *tosses her head, throwing the rat at her. She turns and runs off, screaming*)

DICK. Good old Sukie!

CAPTAIN. Nearly sunk that time, by Neptune!

(*Noises of singing and shouts are heard off* R)

(*In panic*) Oh, don't say she's coming back!

(*The* KING, PING *and* PONG, *with* NATIVE MEN *and* GIRLS *and* SAILORS *enter* R, *singing*)

No—only the Choral Society!

(DICK *slaps him on the back as they both move* L, *and turn, as the singing stops*)

KING. Ho!

DICK. Ko!

KING. Please—why Captain run away?

CAPTAIN. I was afraid—I . . .

KING. 'Fraid?

CAPTAIN. Afraid I'd miss the post!

DICK (*bringing Sukie forward*) Your Majesty—this is my cat, Sukie.

(SUKIE *bows very low*)

She has already caught fifty rats on the island!

KING. Ho! Ko!

PING }
PONG } (*together*) Wallah-wallah—*yassah!*

King. Bravo! Won'ful! Tellum catchum all! No more rats—no more plagues . . .

(*The* Queen *runs in* R)

Captain. Sez you!

(*The* Queen *makes a rapturous approach right to the* Captain, *but the* King *puts his open hand over her face and pushes her back*)

King. Go 'way, 'Orrible! (*To the others*) All is happy 'gain. We make big feast—sing dance! Lettum go altogatha! Ko!

No. 21  *Ensemble* (*The* Company)

*The entire* Company *takes part in a Rumba Number, singing and dancing. The dancing continues as they exit, the singing dies away off as the lights very slowly fade out. Eventually the stage is quite dark and the singing is no longer heard. Beams of light fade in on the stage but not behind the gauze over the gap which has been lowered again.*

A Ballet of Rats *enter to soft music which works up as the dance begins.*

No. 22  *Ballet of Rats*

*At a music cue, the music stops with a cymbal crash. The* Rats *all turn to see* Sukie, *behind the gauze, revealed by spots off* R *and* L. Sukie *leaps up on her hind legs and poses threateningly with her front paws.*

*The* Rats *run off, screaming, to musical effects.*

Black-Out

Sukie *exits in the* Black-Out.

*The music changes during the* Black-Out. Segue *into:*

*The same. Some weeks later, Moonlight.*

*When the lights come up,* Dick *is asleep on the slope up* LC. *A moonbeam on the slope. The skycloth is not lighted and the*

*gap, up* C, *is in complete darkness. The gap should be covered by a gauze.*
*Soft music.* DICK *stirs in his sleep and hums the music softly. Then he awakens slowly, sits up, rubbing his eyes.*

DICK. Alice . . . (*He looks around*) I must have been dreaming. I saw her—heard her—singing.

No. 23 *Song* (DICK *and* ALICE)

(DICK *sings the first verse. Then* ALICE, *unseen, begins to sing the refrain with him. Light is brought up behind the gauze and* ALICE *is seen, standing on a rock above the gap.* DICK *turns and they hold out their arms to each other. The pool of moonlight fades out on Dick as the refrain ends and* ALICE *sings the second verse. The pool on Dick fades in on him as he joins with* ALICE *in the second refrain. As this ends, the light on* ALICE *fades out and she disappears in the darkness.* DICK *sinks down as if about to sleep again. The music continues for a few bars and then fades out. Then lighting very slowly fades in. The birds are heard singing.*

*The* CAPTAIN *is heard singing lustily off* L *and he enters up* C, *from* L. *He checks, seeing Dick*)

CAPTAIN (*shouting jovially*) Ahoy there, me hearty!

(DICK *starts and comes out of his trance*)

DICK. Who's that?

CAPTAIN. Captain Bilge—and a more suitable name I can't imagine!

DICK. I've been dozing.

CAPTAIN. Dozing? Snoring like a duck-billed platypus! Wake up now. Ye look as if ye're half seas over when we should be half over the seas. We sail on the next tide, y'know.

DICK. The next tide? (*He rises*)

CAPTAIN. Aye.

DICK. Good gracious—I'd almost forgotten! We've been here so long, I must be getting used to it.

CAPTAIN. You've done some pretty smart business, young 'un. Alderman Fitzwarren should be mighty grateful to you.

DICK (*smiling*) I hope so. We've opened trade with the Bokos—our future is assured.

CAPTAIN (*with a wink*) And now for the girls we left behind us, eh?

(PANSY, BOTTLE *and the* KING *enter* R, *with the Chorus of* NATIVES. *The* KING *has his arm round Pansy*. BOTTLE *has his arm round a seductive* NATIVE GIRL. *They are all singing*)

No. 24 "THE "GIRL I LEFT BEHIND ME"
(KING, PANSY, BOTTLE *and* NATIVES)

Oh, we're jolly old pals and full of fun
And cling together like the ivy,
For we don't give a darn for anyone
When we keep a date, it's lively!
But now the time has come to part,
We've got to say good-byeeee,
We must each go back to our own sweetheart,
The girl (boy) I left behind me!

(ALL *join in a rousing cheer*)

KING (*to Dick*) So you go now, my friend?

DICK. Alas, yes. We must leave this lovely island, our good friends, and say good-bye.

(*The* QUEEN *rushes on and over to the Captain with outstretched arms*)

QUEEN (*as she crosses*) Aaa-aaaah!

(*The* QUEEN *goes to throw her arms around the* CAPTAIN. *He swings away with a howl into the arms of a Native Girl. He howls and goes* R, *mopping his brow*)

PANSY. Ah, well, we've had a good run, and Bottle is longing to be back on the rolling waves.

BOTTLE. I'd like to have my hand on a rolling-pin!

(SUKIE *enters* C, *and comes down to Dick*)

DICK. Come, Sukie, we must say our farewells.
KING. No! Cat stay! I buy um!

ALL. Yes, keep cat! Cat eat rat! Cat eat rat, so we keep cat!
DICK. Oh, dear! I can't possibly part with Sukie!
QUEEN. Yes, yes! Sell cat! How much?
CAPTAIN. Name your price, me boy. Your fortune's made!
DICK. I *can't!* Sukie's worth more than a King's ransom to me.
CAPTAIN. You'll offend 'em, you know—lose your trade.
KING (*to Dick*) We still have the rats!
PANSY. So has old Bottle.
BOTTLE. Shurrup!
DICK. My cat has killed nearly all the rats for you.
KING. Still some left. Cat go, rats come—more, and more and *more!*

(*The* NATIVES *scream and clamour round Dick and Sukie*)

CAPTAIN (*to Dick; urgently*) You'll have to do something snappy!
DICK. I've got it! (*To the King, holding up his hand*) Don't be afraid—I'll leave my cat with you for a year. I'll lend him!

(*The* NATIVES *cheer*)

KING. No sell?
DICK. No sell—I *lend* him.
QUEEN. Lend Captain, too? I like um!
CAPTAIN. *No!* (*Pointing to Pansy and Bottle*) Lend those two stowaways!
PANSY (*to the Captain*) I don't want to be a loan.
BOTTLE. Sea or no sea, I come with you.
KING (*to Dick*) Is good! When cat kill all rats I make you very rich. I give um treasure *now!* Show in London what King Banga-Banga do! (*He claps his hands*) Slaves —take much gold to ship! Run! Ho! Ko!
PING ⎫ (*together*) Yassah! (*They step forward and pros-*
PONG ⎭ *trate themselves*)
KING. Get canoes! All go to ship!

(PING and PONG *rise and beckon to the others. With a terrific war cry they run off* L)

QUEEN. I come—see um off!

(*The* QUEEN, *with wild whoops runs off after the others.* DICK *takes* SUKIE'S *paw and leads her to the King*)

DICK. Be a good cat, Sukie, and do your duty. We'll come back for you.

(SUKIE *bows to the King and takes her place beside him. The* KING *raises his hat to her*)

Kill all those rats and you can paddle in cream for the rest of your nine lives.

(PANSY *wipes away her tears affectedly*)

CAPTAIN. Tide's in! Show a leg there!
PANSY (*indignantly*) I beg *yours!*
CAPTAIN. It's one and a half bells already. (*He moves to exit but the* KING *checks him*)
KING. Wait! We push your boat out! All my people say farewell! (*Clapping his hands*) Come—to the beaches!

(PING, PONG *and the* NATIVES *run on* L. *The* SAILORS *run on* R)

PING. Canoes ready, massa.

(*Amidst shouting and excited movement, the* COMPANY *forms up to resume the Rumba Number as before. As they are forming up, the* QUEEN *rushes on* L, *wildly excited*)

QUEEN. Dance! Sing! Sing farewell!
KING. Sorry to lose you but glad to see your backs again!
CAPTAIN. Sailors, say your farewells!
SAILORS. Hooray! (*They embrace the Native Girls rapturously*)
CAPTAIN. Oi! Break away!
KING (*leading the Queen forward to the Captain*) You kiss Queen?
CAPTAIN. Not when there's an "R" in the month.

SCENE 3     DICK WHITTINGTON     63

(*To the* SAILORS) Sailors, ban the moats—I mean, man the boats—and away!

DICK. Farewell!

(ALL *sing and dance a reprise of the Rumba refrain*)

No. 24a    *Reprise of No.* 21 (*The* COMPANY)

*They all dance off up* C, *to* R, *except* DICK *and* SUKIE. *The music fades out with the lighting. Only a dim pool of moonlight on Dick up* LC. ALICE *is heard singing refrain of No.* 23. *As this ends, fading out,* DICK *goes up to the gap, his hands outstretched as if Alice were there. Moon spot fades and dawn light on sky-cloth.* DICK *is silhouetted against this as—*

*the* CURTAIN *falls*

# ACT III

## Scene 1

SCENE—*Fitzwarren's Warehouse.*

*When the* CURTAIN *rises,* FREDERICK *is on stage, seated at his desk. The two leading* CLERKS *are also at their desks. Intro. music, at which a number of other* CLERKS *enter* R *and* L. FREDERICK *and the leading* CLERKS *rise and all sing.*

No. 25 *Ensemble* (FREDERICK, KITTY, CLERKS *and* MAIDS)

(*At the second verse,* KITTY, *with some* MAIDS, *enters. She pairs off with* FREDERICK, *and the others pair off with* CLERKS. *The Number ends with a light-hearted Dance, at the end of which all dance off except* FREDERICK *and* KITTY)

KITTY (*in sudden dismay*) Oh dear! I feel *awful!*
FREDERICK. You look all right to *me!*
KITTY (*patting his cheek*) Pet! I meant we ought not to be singing and dancing when we don't know where Dick Whittington and his ship have got to.
FREDERICK. Does seem a bit heartless. Month after month and no news . . .
KITTY. Oh, don't! I can't bear to think of him drowned—and that lovely cat! Poor Sukie! I even feel upset about Pansy and Bottle.
FREDERICK. Oh, come! That's rather overdoing it! Anyway, the Alderman's sure they've all been shipwrecked in a storm—he's telling everyone.
KITTY. Poor Miss Alice—she's drooping about the place like a ghost.
FREDERICK. Well, you'd feel the same if you'd lost me, wouldn't you?
KITTY (*throwing up her chin*) You flatter yourself! (*Moving* L) Miss Alice is *in love!*
FREDERICK (*following to* L) That's what I *mean!*
KITTY (*turning*) I repeat—you flatter yourself!

(KITTY *gives him a little push and exits* L)

FREDERICK (*recovering his balance*) Hey—Kitty! (*Following her*) Wait a minute—Kittee . . . !

(FREDERICK *exits* L.
 *Intro. music to Reprise of No. 23 as* FREDERICK *and* KITTY *exit.*
 ALICE *enters up* R *dressed as for the "vision" in the Island Scene. She comes down slowly*)

ALICE (*sighing*) Oh, Dick! If only I knew what had happened! I can't believe that you are lost—I *can't!* (*She sings*)

  No. 25a *Reprise of No. 23* (ALICE)

(*As she finishes the Number* PERCY *enters* L *and gives a vacuous smile when he sees her alone*)

PERCY. Oh, this is positively *too* heavenly!
ALICE (*coldly*) What is?
PERCY. You, and me—alone.
ALICE. Why?
PERCY. Because you always run away when you see me, as if you're frightened!
ALICE. *Frightened*, Mr Pilbeam?
PERCY. Oh, do call me "Percy"! I mean, dash it, Alice, I *love* you!
ALICE. And I've told you before, I *don't* love you.
PERCY. But I want to marry you!
ALICE. So you've said, and I've said *"no"*!
PERCY. Oh, drat it! You're still thinking of that Whittington fellow!
ALICE. And if I am?
PERCY. It's morbid! He's shipwrecked, so why bother?
ALICE (*turning on him*) You're a heartless beast, and I hate you!
PERCY. But it's true.
ALICE (*trying to stop her tears*) I don't believe it—and anyway, I wouldn't marry you if they *never* came back!

(FITZWARREN *enters and goes to a desk*)

FITZWARREN (*trying to be jovial*) Well, my children, having a little tête-à-tête?

ALICE. *No!* We're *quarrelling!*

(FITZWARREN *looks shocked*)

PERCY. Alice won't believe Dick Whittington's ship is lost—so *trying!*

FITZWARREN (*severely; to Alice*) Nonsense, Alice! The ship's far too long overdue to give any hope. You should get reconciled to it.

PERCY. And marry *me!* That's what I tell her!

FITZWARREN. Of course, of course—and the sooner the better. What do you say, Alice?

ALICE (*angrily*) I say "*No!*"

FITZWARREN (*impatiently*) Then you're a most ungrateful girl!

ALICE. Ungrateful? I don't know what you mean, Father.

(PERCY *looks from one to the other during this altercation, his expression changing comically.* FITZWARREN *takes a large ledger and opens it*)

FITZWARREN (*pointing to some figures*) Look at these figures! The loss of that ship and its cargo has nearly ruined me.

ALICE (*slowly*) Oh. I see what you mean. You want me to marry Percy as a business deal.

PERCY. Oh, positively *yes!* I'm a rattling good investment!

ALICE (*very hurt*) Oh, Father . . .

FITZWARREN (*softening a little*) My dear, don't look like that! There's no harm in having a son-in-law *and* a business partner.

PERCY. Oh, no! Positively *not!* (*He grins at Alice hopefully*)

(ALICE *turns away*)

ALICE. It's no use! In spite of all you say, I still hope that Dick will come back. I must know—for *certain* . . .

(*Distant cheers are heard off.* FREDERICK *enters, very excited*)

FREDERICK (*to Fitzwarren*) Oh, sir—that ship that docked this morning! It's ours!

FITZWARREN. Ours?

FREDERICK. Yes, the *Saucy Sally.*

ALICE (*crying out*) But that was Dick's ship!

FITZWARREN. It can't be!

FREDERICK. It is! The survivors are on their way here! Listen!

(*Sounds of distant cheering*)

They're coming!

ALICE. Dick! Oh, *Dick!*

PERCY. But they're all wrecked—and swimming about—or—or something.

FREDERICK. They're not—they're not! They're getting a terrific welcome! Listen to it!

(*The cheering gets nearer still.*

*The* CROWD *enters up* L, *shouting and cheering.* BOTTLE, PANSY *and* CAPTAIN BILGE, *dressed in rags, are carried on the shoulders of some of the* CLERKS. *They are singing a sea shanty. Suggested Number:* "*We Be Three Poor Mariners*")

CAPTAIN (*leaping down*) Ahoy, there! The Navy's here —or a bit of it!

(ALICE *scans their faces anxiously, too overwrought to speak for the moment*)

FITZWARREN. Well, well! This is beyond belief!

PERCY. We thought you were *drowned!* Oh, it's too bad!

CAPTAIN. Not us! We landed bang on a desert island.

ALICE. Yes, but where is . . . ?

BOTTLE (*boastfully; ignoring Alice*) Blowed a hundred miles off the map by a tycoon.

PANSY. Been playing Robinson Crusoe ever since!

ALICE. But where are the—the others?
CAPTAIN. We're all here, my dear, all here—all here.
CROWD. Hooray!

(*There is general chatter and laughter as the* CROWD *gathers round the three admiringly.* ALICE *is distracted with anxiety and tries to break in*)

PANSY. Talk about adventures! *I* could tell you some things . . . !
ALICE (*wringing her hands*) I want to know about . . .
CROWD. Tell us! Go on!
CAPTAIN. Laugh! You'd ha' died! (*Roaring with laughter*) Pansy mistook a crocodile's back for a washing board!
PANSY (*to the Captain*) And I mistook you for Tarzan! As for Bottle—remember that abandoned old cove?
BOTTLE (*turning on her indignantly*) Who's an abandoned old cove?
ALICE. Oh, please—*please* . . .
FITZWARREN. What about the ship?
CAPTAIN. Salvaged, patched up, good as new!
BOTTLE. Pansy's petticoats for sails—and . . .
PANSY (*interrupting*) All right, no details!
ALICE. Captain Bilge! (*Pulling at the Captain's sleeve*) Captain Bilge! Please tell me—where is Dick Whittington?

(*The* CAPTAIN *pauses in his laughter and chatter for a moment and looks at her as if collecting his thoughts*)

CAPTAIN. Dick Whittington? Oh, we lost *him!*

(*The* CAPTAIN *turns back to the others and resumes the chatter.* ALICE *turns away, despairingly*)

ALICE. Lost! Then there's nothing left to hope for! (*After a moment's pause she moves to Fitzwarren*) Father!
FITZWARREN. What is it, Alice?
ALICE. You were right. Dick has—gone.
FITZWARREN (*kindly*) I was afraid so, my dear.
ALICE. So—if I must—I will do as you wish and marry Mr Pilbeam.

FITZWARREN. Sensible girl! All for the best! (*He pats her hand understandingly*) I'll announce it at once. No time like the present!

(*As* FITZWARREN *turns to the Crowd,* ALICE *turns away with a little gesture of resignation*)

ALICE. I don't care what happens—nothing matters now!

FITZWARREN (*holding up his hand for silence*) Ladies and gentlemen, this is a great day for the House of Fitzwarren! We welcome our shipwrecked friends and have happy news to greet them! I am delighted to announce the betrothal of my daughter Alice to Mr Percy Pilbeam!

PANSY (*to Bottle*) I told you so—I felt it in me bones!

(ALL *cheer*)

CROWD (*ad lib.*) Congratulations! Hope you'll be happy! (*Etc.*)

(ALICE *smiles wanly as* FITZWARREN *leads her to Percy*)

PERCY (*giggling inanely*) Oh, I say! This is positively—I mean—(*to Alice*) what about a kiss *now*?

ALICE (*drawing back*) *No*, Mr Pilbeam!

PERCY. Call me "Percy".

ALICE (*stubbornly*) No, Mr Pilbeam!

CAPTAIN. Let's have a slap-up party to celebrate.

PANSY. I'll do me hula-hula. (*She does a few steps*)

BOTTLE. I'll recite! (*Declaims*) "It was the scooter Hesperus . . ."

PANSY (*interrupting*) No, thank you—we've suffered enough!

FITZWARREN. We'll have a grand wedding and invite you all to it! (*To Alice*) Come, my dear! Forget the past and be happy!

(KITTY *and* MAIDS *enter* L, *to renewed cheers and* "*wolf*" *whistles*)

CAPTAIN. Come along, girls!

No. 26   *Ensemble Chorus* (*The* COMPANY)

(ALL *form a half-circle round Alice and Percy for the Number*)

FREDERICK. Three cheers for the happy pair—Miss Alice and Mr Pilbeam!

(PERCY *takes Alice's hand possessively, as all cheer. During this speech* DICK *appears* L. *He is very ragged, as he was in Scene* 1. *He stands quite still, taking in the significance of the scene. Then* ALICE *turns and sees him.* ALL *turn as they see her gazing, as if frozen. There is a sudden silence as* ALL *follow her gaze*)

ALICE (*with a little sob*) Dick! Oh, Dick!

ALICE *tries to take a step forward and collapses at the feet of Fitzwarren. Hold tableau as*—

*the* TABS *close*

*In Front of* TABS:
No. 27 *Speciality Number* (PERCY *and* DANCING GIRLS)

## SCENE 2

SCENE—*Fitzwarren's Warehouse.*

*When the* TABS *open,* FREDERICK *and the* CLERKS *are at their desks as before.*

No. 28 *Reprise of No.* 6

*Trio* (FREDERICK *and* CLERKS *with Chorus of* KITTY, MAIDS *and* CLERKS)
(*To music—as in Act I,* FREDERICK *turns, comes down* C *to steps as previously*)

FREDERICK.
    Life's still obscure,
    Opportunities are fewer,
    The books of the firm need revision—
CLERK (R)
CLERK (L) } (*shouting, without turning*)
    Revision!

FREDERICK. There's little in the till
CLERKS (*turning*)
>And the dividends are nil—
FREDERICK.
>For there's much more subtraction then division!
ALL (*spoken sepulchrally*)
>Oh dear—dear—dear—dear—dear—dear—*dear!*

(*The two* CLERKS *slip off their stools and join Frederick* C)

ALL (*singing*)
>Insolvency—care—
>Is pervading Golden Square,
>When ships sink at sea, it's the devil!

CLERK (R)
>So for Arcady we pine,

CLERK (L)
>And a cup of cowslip wine,

ALL.
>As we join the Fairy Folk in a revel!

(ALL *dance round the stage to* "*Spring Song*", *scattering flowers right and left as before. Finish* C, *and sing repeat of refrain*)

>But such happiness
>We can hardly so express
>And keep Fitzwarren's books in addition! (*Pause*)

FREDERICK (*on an upward scale; anxiously watched by the others*) Ah-ha-di-hi-hi-hi-tion!

(ALL *do the* "*winning boxer's sign*")

ALL (*sung*)
>Though we stand on Ruin's brink
>Yet we'll stick to quills and ink,
>Instead of a Fairy Expedition!

(*They all start to return to their desks with bowed heads and clasped hands, when the Chorus of* CLERKS, KITTY *and* MAIDS *all dance in to* "*Spring Song*" *music, and the dance is repeated as in Act I.* FREDERICK *and the two* CLERKS *join in the dance as if in a trance. The dance is deliberately burlesqued. As it approaches the end,* DICK *enters* L, *and watches the last few bars, exasperated. The dance ends.* ALL *look at Dick*)

DICK. Upon my word! Wasting time again!

(FREDERICK, R, *gives a peal of high-pitched laughter and collapses backwards. He is caught by the two* CLERKS *who are standing on each side of and slightly behind him*)

FREDERICK (*recovering*) Enter the slave-driver!

DICK. This is disgraceful!

CLERKS (*speaking glumly; in unison*) Beg pardon, Mr Whittington.

KITTY }
MAIDS } (*ditto*) Sorreh, we're sure!

(KITTY *and the* MAIDS *tilt up their chins and exit up* L. *The* CLERKS *all sidle up stage into little groups, whispering together*)

DICK (*moving* C) There's a lot to be done this morning —a *lot!*

FREDERICK. *As* usual! (*Moving to Dick*) What's the matter with you, Dick? You've worked like a fiend since you came back.

DICK. I want to make the business prosperous again. That shipwreck nearly killed it.

FREDERICK. It wasn't *your* fault.

DICK. I lost the cargo—worth a mint of money.

FREDERICK. But trade's better now. Relax!

DICK. I've another reason for working.

FREDERICK. A-ha! Now we have it!

(FREDERICK *winks at the* CLERKS *who echo "A-ha!" to each other as they move down stage in groups*)

FREDERICK. Pilbeam versus Whittington, eh?

DICK (*laughing*) Perhaps!

(ALICE *enters down* R. *She pauses as she sees the Clerks*)

ALICE. Oh. (*She takes a few steps forward and hesitates*)

FREDERICK. Come in, Miss Alice! Excuse us, won't you? (*He makes beckoning gestures to the Clerks*) We've

## SCENE 2   DICK WHITTINGTON   73

got a new cargo to check—*outside!* (*He bows to Alice and goes up* R)

(*The* CLERKS *grin and wink, then follow* FREDERICK *off up* R)

DICK. Alice! Why do you look at me so strangely?

ALICE. Because I am trying to see you as a stranger.

DICK. I—a stranger?

ALICE. I must! When they said you were lost I thought they meant—drowned! (*She breaks off unhappily*)

DICK (*gently; moving to her*) You were not to know that I had merely lost my way in the maze of streets round the docks.

ALICE. But I should never have promised to marry Percy! Oh, how foolish I was!

DICK. It was understandable. He caught you on the rebound! (*He grins wryly*)

ALICE. I can't marry him—it's *impossible!*

DICK (*hopefully*) Perhaps he'll release you . . .

ALICE. He won't! It's father.

DICK. Did you ask him?

ALICE. Yes, and he gave me a long lecture about the honour of the Fitzwarren's! I've *got* to marry Percy, even if it wrecks our lives!

DICK. Surely, if we love each other, *nothing* can come between us!

(*They sing*)

No. 29 *Reprise Duet* (ALICE *and* DICK)

(*At the end of the Number they embrace.* FITZWARREN *enters and sees them. He looks at them angrily*)

FITZWARREN. Alice! Dick! What is the meaning of this?

(FITZWARREN *advances to* C, *as they break apart guiltily*)

DICK. I'm sorry, Alderman . . .

ALICE (*defiantly*) And I'm *not* sorry, so there!

FITZWARREN. I don't understand you, Alice.

ALICE. No—if you did you would know that I love Dick.

DICK. Alice wants to be released from her engagement to Pilbeam.

FITZWARREN. This is preposterous! I won't hear of it!

ALICE. I don't love Percy—I don't want him

FITZWARREN. You can't break a promise.

DICK. But if Pilbeam doesn't mind . . . ?

FITZWARREN (*facing Dick*) You are still not in a position to keep my daughter, young man!

DICK. Since I have been home the business has prospered, Alderman. I have almost retrieved your losses.

ALICE. Dick has worked hard.

FITZWARREN (*impatiently*) Yes—yes, I know that. I hope I am just. I have given you back your old position of trust, Dick, but that doesn't make you a rich man.

ALICE (*hotly*) I'd marry Dick if he were in the gutter!

FITZWARREN. Nonsense!

DICK. I may yet be a wealthy man, Alderman.

FITZWARREN. *You*—a City clerk? Tush!

DICK. Some day my cat will come home with a fortune.

ALICE. Oh, yes! I'd almost forgotten Sukie!

FITZWARREN. So your fortune depends on a cat? Ridiculous! (*He laughs sarcastica"y*)

DICK (*proudly*) My future has always depended on my cat! It was the prophecy of the Bow Bells! Some day I shall be Lord Mayor of London—Sir Richard Whittington!

ALICE. Oh, Dick! How wonderful!

FITZWARREN. I'll hear no more of it! (*To Alice*) Back to your room, Alice. I have work to do.

(ALICE *pauses defiantly for a moment, then with a glance and a smile at Dick, she exits* R)

(*To Dick*) Enough of this daydreaming! Remember, my daughter is the future Mrs Pilbeam. If you value your position here, leave her alone.

(*After a moment's hesitation,* DICK *turns on his heel*)

SCENE 2         DICK WHITTINGTON         75

DICK. I'll remember, Alderman.

(DICK *exits* L.

FITZWARREN *turns and goes to Frederick's desk, up* C)

FITZWARREN (*as he goes*) I don't know what the young people are coming to nowadays—no sense of responsibility! All wanting to rush into unsuitable marriages . . .

(FITZWARREN, *still muttering, sits at the desk up* C, *with only his back showing. He is poring over a ledger.*
FREDERICK *and* KITTY *enter* L. *They are arm in arm*)

KITTY (*with a long, deep sigh*) Oh, Frederick!

(FITZWARREN *starts and glares round at them but they do not see him*)

Say it again—just like you did before!

FREDERICK. I love you!

(*They cross slowly to* R *as they are talking*)

KITTY (*sighing ecstatically*) Again!

FREDERICK. I love you, I love you, I love you! Is that enough?

(FITZWARREN *shakes his head and holds it as if in agony*)

KITTY. Oh, no! I could listen to it for ever!

(FITZWARREN *crouches and covers his ears*)

FREDERICK. Then marry me, Kitty darling!

KITTY (*simulating surprise*) Oh, Frederick! You do sweep a girl off her feet! I'd no idea . . .

FREDERICK (*bewildered*) No idea? Well! *Women!*

(*They sit down* R)

KITTY. Tell me again.

(*They gaze into each other's eyes and murmur.*
PANSY *and* BOTTLE *enter up* R)

BOTTLE. Well, what abaht it?
PANSY. What about what?
BOTTLE. What abaht what abaht what?
PANSY. What about what you was saying?

(*They walk slowly to* L *as they talk and* FITZWARREN *looks round furiously*)

BOTTLE. Oh, come orf it! *You* know!
PANSY. Not being physic, I *don't!*
BOTTLE. You said we'd been tied up so long we might as well get spliced.
PANSY (*fluttering her eyelids at him*) Oh, Mr Bottle! Is this a proposal?
BOTTLE (*reluctantly*) In a manner o' speaking—if you like to put it that way—yes!

(FITZWARREN *shakes his fist at them, but they do not see him.* PANSY *and* BOTTLE *sit down* L)

PANSY (*determined to be romantic*) Coo—what romance! It's sent me all shivery down me backbone! (*She suddenly turns on Bottle, hugging and kissing him.*

(BOTTLE *gasps and struggles*)

Oh, you great big beautiful Bottle!
BOTTLE (*fighting free*) Oh! Give over, do!
KITTY. Oh, Frede*rick!*
FREDERICK. Now all we have to do——
KITTY. —is to ask the Alderman——
PANSY (*shouting triumphantly*) —for time off to get married! Whoopee!
BOTTLE. I bet he'll say . . .
FITZWARREN (*shouting*) *No!*

(*The four jump and look round startled as* FITZWARREN *rises and comes down* C)

What do you mean by coming in here and behaving like this? It's *disgraceful!*
KITTY. W-w-well!
FREDERICK. I didn't see *him!*
PANSY. That's torn it!
BOTTLE. Hoppin' mad, he is!
FITZWARREN. How dare you waste time like this? I pay you to *work!* (*Striding up and down angrily*) Time off

Scene 2        DICK WHITTINGTON        77

to get married, indeed! I never heard of such impudence!

(DICK *enters excitedly* L)

DICK. Excuse me, sir.
FITZWARREN (*turning sharply*) Yes? What is it now?
DICK. Some important guests have arrived—the King and Queen of the Boko Islands!
FITZWARREN. Good gracious me! And no civic welcome!

(*Triumphal music.* PING *and* PONG *walk in backwards, bowing as they come. They back into Pansy and Bottle on one side, and Frederick and Kitty on the other.*
*The* KING *and* QUEEN *enter, gorgeously dressed. They pause for effect before coming down* C. *They are followed by* CAPTAIN BILGE)

KING. Walla-walla-bong!
QUEEN. Dinga-dinga-dong!
CAPTAIN. That's French for "wotcher"!
FITZWARREN (*bowing solemnly to the King and Queen*) Greetings, your Majesties.

(*The* KING *and* QUEEN *bow once again in return.* PING *and* PONG *rub their foreheads on the ground.* FITZWARREN *again bows and the bows are repeated ad lib. until the* CAPTAIN *intervenes*)

CAPTAIN (*roaring*) Stand at—*ease!*

(*They all stop with a jerk.* PING *and* PONG *leap to their feet with a yell.*
ALICE *enters* R)

ALICE (*very excitedly*) Oh, Dick—Father! It's Sukie—she's come back!

(*Repeat of triumphal music.*
SUKIE *enters* L, *and pauses for effect before coming down. She is hung with jewels and looks very sleek and prosperous. Behind her come two* SLAVES *staggering under the weight of a* "*treasure chest*".
*A* CROWD *enters*)

CROWD (*ad lib.*) It's the cat! Dick Whittington's wonderful cat! (*Etc.*)

KING (*with a sweeping gesture towards Sukie*) Wallawalla! King Cat!

(*The* QUEEN *rushes to* SUKIE *and embraces her. She disengages her in a very dignified manner and twirls her whiskers, looking round confidently*)

QUEEN. Blinkin' good cat! She killum rats—all dead!

(DICK *goes to Sukie and pats her.* SUKIE *miaouws and makes a great fuss of Dick*)

DICK. Bravo, Sukie! Good cat!

FITZWARREN. Astonishing animal!

(SUKIE *goes to* ALICE *who pats her*)

ALICE. Oh, Sukie! *Dear* Sukie!

CAPTAIN. She's done the *cat* trick! (*He roars with laughter*)

(*The* KING *goes to the treasure chest which the* SLAVES *put* C. *He opens the lid and brings out a handful of gold and jewels*)

KING. See! Gold—silver—diamonds—for Dick Whittington.

DICK (*astonished*) For *me?*

QUEEN (*chuckling*) For cat's master! Good cat—eatum rats!

ALICE. Oh, Dick, what a handsome reward!

KING (*going to Fitzwarren and tapping him on the chest to emphasize his words*) Dick Whittington fine chap! You lucky boss! Me trade with *Dick*—he rich mans!

CROWD (*cheering*) Bravo, Dick!

BOTTLE. I always *did* like that lad!

(DICK *and* ALICE *are* C *together, looking in amazement at the treasure*)

FITZWARREN. Bless my soul! Dick has made a name for himself!

CAPTAIN. Aye—our Dick's a hero! He deserves a medal!
FREDERICK. Give him a medal!
CLERKS. Give him a medal!
FITZWARREN (*to the Clerks*) I promise you he shall have civic honours!
1ST CLERK. Make him a Liveryman——
2ND CLERK. —a Councillor——
3RD CLERK. —an Alderman——
4TH CLERK. —a Sheriff——
ALL. And Lord Mayor of London!

(ALL *cheer and* DICK *smiles*)

FITZWARREN. This is a great honour for us! It is not every day that we entertain royalty!

(*He beams at the* KING *and* QUEEN, *and they all bow to each other again*)

We should like you to stay to my daughter's wedding.

(DICK *and* ALICE *look at each other in dismay*)

DICK. Alice . . .
ALICE. My wedding! I'd almost forgotten!
QUEEN. Wedding—ho, ko!
KING. Big feast! Yassah!

(*The* KING *and* QUEEN *look at each other and rub their stomachs appreciatively*)

KING (*to Fitzwarren*) We come, Big Chief!

(*The* CROWD *are laughing and talking.*
PERCY *rushes on* L. *He is waving a letter and seems very perturbed*)

PANSY. Here comes Mother's Handsome!
PERCY. I say—look! I mean, dash it all!
FITZWARREN. Just in time to receive royal congratulations, my boy.
PERCY. But I can't! I've got a letter from a suer . . .
FITZWARREN. *What?*

PERCY. I mean, Rosie's father. He's going to sue me for breach of promise.

PANSY. What ever made you promise to marry *him?*

DICK (*quickly*) What's all this about, Percy?

PERCY. I'd clean forgotten I'd given Rosie a ring!

FITZWARREN (*wrathfully*) D'you mean to say you're really engaged to another girl, sir?

PERCY (*shrinking back*) Y-y-yes! Her p-pater's p-positively p-palpitating with p-passion!

ALICE (*joyfully*) I'll release you, Percy. You're quite free!

PERCY. Free? Don't I even fetch half price?

ALICE. You are *free!*

PERCY. Alice! Of course, I'm afraid it will break your heart . . .

FITZWARREN. I could break your head!

ALICE (*to Fitzwarren*) Father, if my heart *is* broken, you alone can mend it! (*She takes Dick by the hand*)

DICK (*boldly*) Alderman Fitzwarren, have I your permission to marry your daughter?

FITZWARREN (*laughing*) You win, Dick! Take her, my boy, and be happy!

(*Bow Bells in the distance.* DICK *and* ALICE *embrace. The others cheer and shout congratulations.* SUKIE *goes to them and hugs them both*)

DICK. Good old Sukie!

(*The chimes get louder*)

Bow bells!

(DICK *and* SUKIE *look at each other*)

ALICE. "Turn again, Whittington, thrice Lord Mayor of London!"

(ALICE *holds out her hands to* DICK *and he takes them in his*)

Sir Richard Whittington—my brave knight!

(*The Full* COMPANY *enters*)

ALL. Sir Richard Whittington!

(ALL *group and sing*)

No. 30 *Grand Finale* (FULL COMPANY)
*Reprise of Bow Bells*

CURTAIN

Any character costumes or wigs needed in the performance of this play can be hired from CHARLES H. FOX Ltd, 25 Shelton Street, London WC2H 9HX

# FURNITURE AND PROPERTY LIST

## ACT I

### Scene 1

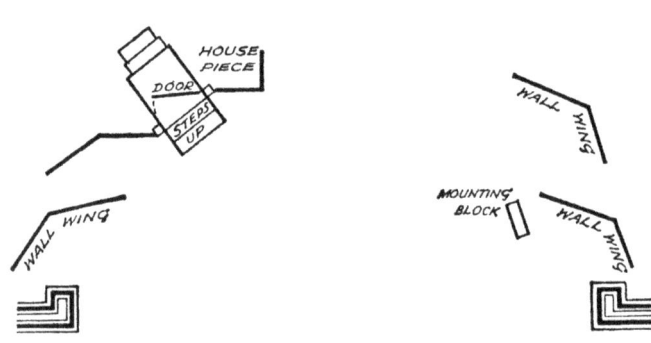

*On stage:* Mounting block

*Off stage:* Pack (DICK)
Bladders on sticks, long feathers, comic hats and masks (REVELLERS)

### Scene 2

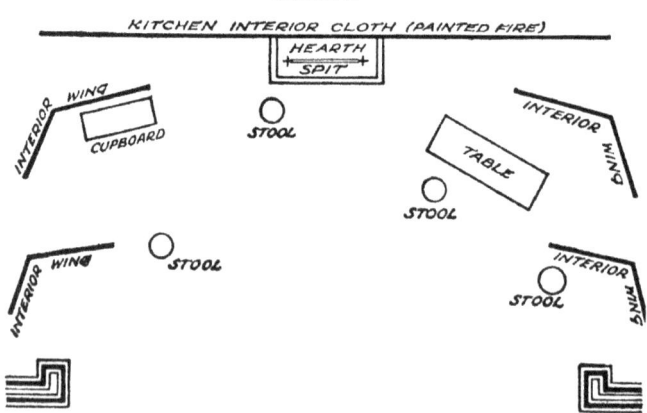

# DICK WHITTINGTON

*On stage:* Table. *On it:* rolling-pin, pastry-board, tankard, cleaning rag
Kitchen range with spit
Cupboard. *In it:* slab of "pastry"
4 stools

*Off stage:* Dusters, brooms, brushes (CHORUS)

SCENE 3

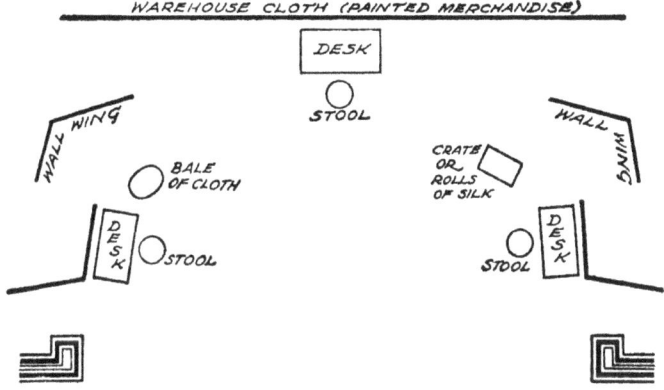

*On stage:* Desk (up C) *On it:* ledger, quill
Desk (R) *On it:* ledger, quill
Desk (L) *On it:* ledger, quill
3 stools
Bale of cloth
Crate or rolls of silk or cloth

*Off stage:* Rolling-pin (PANSY)
3 rats (SUKIE)

*Personal:* PERCY: quizzing-glass

SCENE 4

*On stage:* Milestone

*Off stage:* Stick and bundle (DICK)


ACT II

SCENE 1

Setting as Act I, Scene 3
*Set:* Bales of materials and lengths of silk, etc.

*Off stage:* Papers (DICK)
Sea chest. *In it:* picture in folding case (DICK)
Length of thin rope (DICK)


SCENE 2

*On stage:* Coil of rope

*Off stage:* Telescope (CAPTAIN)
Copies of music (SAILORS)
Large tuning-fork (CAPTAIN)
Small saucepans and metal ladles (PING and PONG)
Shields and spears

*Personal:* CAPTAIN: red handkerchief

## Scene 3

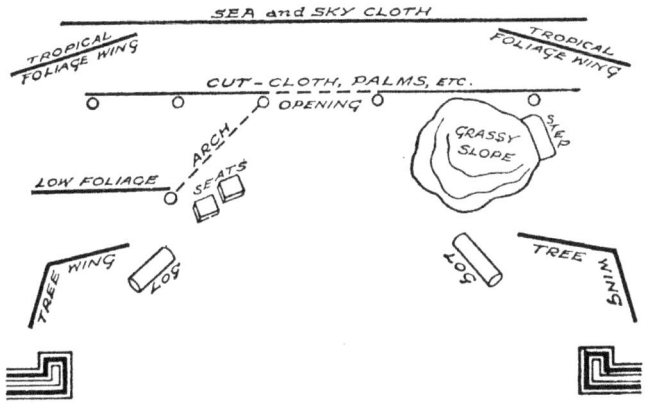

*On stage:* 2 seats
2 logs

*Off stage:* Palm leaf fans (CHORUS)

## ACT III

### Scene 1

Setting as Act I, Scene 3

### Scene 2

Setting as previous scene
*Off stage:* Treasure chest. *In it:* gold and jewels (SLAVES)
Jewels (SUKIE)
Letter (PERCY)

# EFFECTS PLOT

## ACT I

### Scene 1

*Cue* 1    Reprise of No. 1    (Page 3)
*New Year bells peal out*

### Scene 2

*No cues*

### Scene 3

*No cues*

### Scene 4

*Cue* 2    Sukie droops. There is a pause    (Page 27)
*Sound of Bow Bells*

*Cue* 3    Dick: ". . . the bells come true!"    (Page 28)
*Cut Bow Bells*

*Cue* 4    Dick and Sukie exit    (Page 28)
*Bow Bells ring out*

## ACT II

### Scene 1

*No cues*

### Interlude

*No cues*

## Scene 2

| | | |
|---|---|---|
| Cue 5 | The TABS open<br>*Sound of wind and thunder* | (Page 40) |
| Cue 6 | SAILORS: "Hooray!"<br>*Wind and distant thunder* | (Page 40) |
| Cue 7 | PANSY: ". . . to stow away!"<br>*Wind and thunder* | (Page 41) |
| Cue 8 | BOTTLE: ". . . trouble *at all*!"<br>*Wind, thunder and lightning* | (Page 41) |
| Cue 9 | 4TH SAILOR: "Long way to go, chum!"<br>*Wind and thunder* | (Page 41) |
| Cue 10 | PANSY: ". . . not *quite sure!*"<br>*Thunder—wind howls* | (Page 41) |
| Cue 11 | PANSY: ". . . yourself—like *me.*"<br>*Thunder* | (Page 41) |
| Cue 12 | PANSY: ". . . cost you something!"<br>*Wind and thunder* | (Page 42) |
| Cue 13 | CAPTAIN: ". . . choppy at times . . ."<br>*Sudden howl of wind* | (Page 45) |
| Cue 14 | CAPTAIN: ". . . good to watch them."<br>*A bell sounds* | (Page 46) |
| Cue 15 | CAPTAIN strikes deck with tuning-fork<br>*Loud wailing "ping" is heard* | (Page 48) |
| Cue 16 | DICK: ". . . task of expanding."<br>*Sharp bang is heard* | (Page 50) |

## Interlude

*No cues*

## Scene 3

*No cues*

## ACT III

### SCENE 1

*No cues*

### SCENE 2

*Cue* 17   FITZWARREN: "... and be happy!"   (Page 80)
           *Distant Bow Bells*

*Cue* 18   DICK: "Good old Sukie!"   (Page 80)
           *The chimes get louder*

www.ingramcontent.com/pod-product-compliance
Ingram Content Group UK Ltd.
Pitfield, Milton Keynes, MK11 3LW, UK
UKHW021844210426
5322IPUK00022B/449